ANTHONY EDEN

ANTHONY EDEN

SIDNEY ASTER

INTRODUCTION BY
A. J. P. TAYLOR

WEIDENFELD AND NICOLSON
LONDON

To my parents
Ida and Sam

Designed by Behram Kapadia
for George Weidenfeld and Nicolson Ltd
11 St John's Hill, London SW11

ISBN 0 297 77123 X

Printed and bound in Great Britain by
Morrison & Gibb Ltd, London and Edinburgh

Extracts from Lord Avon's memoirs are quoted
by kind permission of the publishers,
Cassell and Company Ltd.

CONTENTS

ILLUSTRATIONS

INTRODUCTION

ANTHONY EDEN was for most of his political life a man of promise, named as the future prime minister by Stanley Baldwin, Neville Chamberlain and Winston Churchill. Many such prophecies are made, and few fulfilled. In Eden's case the promise came true to his misfortune and that of the country. Eden's policy during his ten years as foreign secretary was marked by caution, high principle and rigid adherence to diplomatic rectitude. No man was more skilful at drafting a pact or a protocol; no man more reluctant to take decisive action. Throughout the 1930s he championed the League of Nations and was the hero of the League of Nations Union. During the Second World War he tempered Churchill's rash impulses and secured good relations even with Soviet Russia. After the war he successfully directed the conference at Geneva which ended the French war in Vietnam. His reputation as a peacemaker stood high.

Within less than two years as prime minister Eden had destroyed this reputation and led Great Britain to one of the greatest humiliations in her history. Faced with Nasser's nationalization of the Suez Canal, Eden seemed to take on a new personality. He acted impatiently and on impulse. Previously flexible he now relied on dogma, denouncing Nasser as a second Hitler. Though he claimed to be upholding international law, he in fact disregarded the United Nations Organization which he had helped to create. He deceived the Americans whose friendship he had always made the cornerstone of his policy. He conspired – there is no other word – with the French and Israelis and launched a surprise attack on Egypt, designed to seize the Suez Canal by force. Eden if anyone, not Nasser, was the Hitler of 1956 with the same cloud of words and the same unscrupulousness of action. To crown all the attack was badly prepared and conducted. It ended in complete failure. Soon afterwards ill health compelled Eden to resign. The consequences of his folly and wilfulness are still to be seen in the Middle East.

What can account for such a reversal of policy and character? Perhaps Eden's stock of patience had been exhausted during the years when he pressed this quality on others. Perhaps, living for so long under Churchill's shadow, he too aspired to be a dynamic leader. Or, on a more prosaic note, his rashness may have been a preliminary symptom of the illness that was to strike him down. The problem is beyond the wit of man to solve. The outcome was pathetic rather than tragic. Eden had many great qualities and some diplomatic successes. But he will be remembered as the prime minister who steered the ship of state on to the rocks.

A. J. P. TAYLOR

I

THE EARLY YEARS
1897-1931

ANTHONY EDEN was among the shortest-serving British prime
ministers in the twentieth century. Only Andrew Bonar Law and
Sir Alec Douglas-Home held office for briefer periods. First elected
as a member of parliament in 1923, Eden held the position of
foreign secretary for more than ten years, and succeeded Winston
Churchill as prime minister on 6 April 1955. He resigned because
of ill-health on 9 January 1957. In that short time he had tragically
illustrated the truth in his favourite observation by Lord Acton:
'Ideals in politics are never realized, but the pursuit of them
determines history.'

Robert Anthony Eden was born on 12 June 1897, ten days before
Queen Victoria's Diamond Jubilee. His birthplace was Windlestone Hall, near Bishop Auckland in Durham, the chief seat of the
Eden family for more than 300 years. Family genealogy traces their
ancestry back to a Robert Eden, born during the long reign of
Edward III, and who is known to have died in 1413, two years before
the battle of Agincourt. The Eden line flourished and grew in
landed wealth and influence. In 1672 Charles II conferred on them
their first baronetcy, that of West Auckland. The family's responsibilities and interests widened, and a tradition was established
which identified particularly with the fields of foreign affairs and
social reform.

Among the more eminent members of the Eden family was
William Eden, first Baron Auckland. He was an eighteenth-century

penal reformer who established the National Bank of Ireland and held several diplomatic posts abroad and Cabinet positions at home. His nephew, Sir Frederick Morton Eden, was an economist and early sociologist who published in 1797 *The State of the Poor*, a pioneering work later praised by Karl Marx. Sir Robert Eden, a brother of Lord Auckland, became the last colonial governor of Maryland and gave the family another baronetcy, that of Maryland, which King George III bestowed in 1776. Sir Robert's marriage to Caroline Calvert conferred on all his descendants the curious status of counts and countesses of the Holy Roman Empire. Anthony Eden's forbears included members of parliament, two bishops, an ambassador to Berlin and Vienna, a governor-general of India, a lieutenant-governor of Bengal, and an early nineteenth-century novelist, Emily Eden. His grandfather, Sir William Eden, retired to Windlestone Hall to lead the life of a country gentleman.

Such was the ancestry into which Anthony Eden was born. He joined in the nursery a sister, Marjorie, aged ten, and two brothers, John, aged eight, and Timothy, aged four. A fifth child, Nicholas, was born three years later. Much of the Eden inheritance, formidable and overpowering, was epitomized in the character of Anthony Eden's father, Sir William Eden, seventh Baronet of West Auckland and fifth Baronet of Maryland. In 1886 he had married Lady Sybil Frances Grey, who was descended from the prime minister in office at the time of the parliamentary reform act of 1832.

It was Anthony Eden's brother, Timothy, successor to the family titles, who left information about Sir William to posterity. In 1933 Sir Timothy, as he then was, published a life of his father, *The Tribulations of a Baronet*. In this revealing piece of family biography, he described a handsome and passionate man with an overabundance of talent and temper. Educated at Eton, Sir William then served in the army, rising to the rank of colonel. His adult life was devoted to managing an estate of over 8000 acres and presiding over the life of his family. Besides being a sportsman and master of the South Durham hounds, he was a collector of French impressionist paintings before they became fashionable. After his death a trustee, Lord Derby, was so outraged by the strangeness of the collection that he ordered them to be sold. Sir William himself was an accomplished artist in watercolours, exhibiting at the progressive New English Art Club, the Royal Institute of Painters in Watercolours, and at the Salon, Champs de Mars in Paris. But his talents were overshadowed by a remarkable eccentricity and storms of temper. As a parent he could not endure for long the presence of his own children. He inspired the coldest respect and discouraged any form of intimacy, which left him in old age a sad, lonely man.

Life at Windlestone Hall followed the style typical of upper-class country life just preceding World War I. There was an endless coming and going of visitors against the continuous background of servants, gardeners, grooms and keepers of the estate going about their work. Such surroundings offered excitement and opportunities to the Eden children. The spacious beauty of the countryside was theirs to explore, and country sports were easily accessible – though Anthony Eden himself never excelled at either riding or shooting. From his mother, a famous beauty painted by James Whistler, he acquired elegance and charm. She recalled in later years that he was always the quiet, kind one of her family, and quite unmischievous. Childhood photographs depict him as a delicate, slender figure, almost feminine in good looks, with full cheeks, sensitive eyes, and wavy hair brushed in a fringe across his forehead.

It was from Sir William, however, that Anthony Eden's character received its lasting traits. He inherited his father's strong temper, which only the immense discipline of self-control kept in check. His colleagues of later years amply testified to the rare outbursts of irritation which relieved moments of tension. While there was no intimacy, there existed between father and son genuine respect. Courage and honesty were qualities which the ambivalent Sir William could easily pass on. So too was a certain idiosyncrasy of dress which caught the public attention when his son first took major office. In later years Anthony Eden's affection for his father increased, as did his admiration for Sir William's watercolours, which decorated his rooms at Oxford and even hung for a short time at 10 Downing Street.

The informal instruction which Anthony Eden received at Windlestone included an early introduction to art appreciation, particularly the French impressionists. A grounding in French and German was given by a governess. This was supplemented by frequent visits to the continent, mainly to France and Germany, and for a time Anthony Eden spoke French more easily than English. When he turned eight he was sent as a day boy to the South Kensington Preparatory School in London. Although he had

3

difficulty with mathematics, his headmaster reported his general conduct to be excellent. The following year, 1906, he was sent to Sandroyd School near Cobham in Surrey, where he stayed for four years. This was a well-known, fashionable school, the orthodox entrance to the privileges of an education at Eton and Oxford. At Sandroyd he won prizes for French and history, and managed to overcome his weakness in mathematics. His English master reported that he would prove to be a strong as well as a lovable character.

In January 1911 Anthony Eden went up to Eton. He joined the house of Ernest Lee Churchill, popularly known as 'Jelly', which had a reputation for athletic distinction. The four years that Anthony Eden spent at Eton were not particularly happy or fruitful ones. He was a sensitive, somewhat lonely figure, whose strengths were kindness and thoughtfulness towards others. His next older brother, Timothy, had taken his share of prizes and had been a keen athlete at the school. The outstanding feature – if it can be called such – of Anthony Eden's years at the school was that he made no distinct impression either on his contemporaries or his masters. Some recall that he was a well-dressed and handsome boy, generally liked and respected, but most agree that he was inconspicuous. His academic record indicates that he made steady progress, and depicts him as a conscientious worker capable of application. At games he was a good all-rounder, gaining house colours for football and showing promise as an oarsman. He developed at Eton those characteristics most commonly associated with him in later years: sincerity, public spirit, a capacity for taking trouble, and a good, though not high-powered, intellect.

On 28 June 1914 Anthony Eden was on the Thames at Eton, being coached at rowing, when he heard the news of the assassination of the Archduke Franz Ferdinand at Sarajevo. He had just turned seventeen and for the first time in his life began to keep a diary. In it he wrote of the outbreak of World War I, and from newspaper accounts he followed political and military events as the ghastly toll of carnage mounted on the continent. His last year at Eton had been particularly unhappy, marked by personal bereavement. His brother Timothy, who had been travelling in Germany when war broke out on 4 August, was interned. After spending two years as a prisoner, he was released and then commissioned as a lieutenant in the Yorkshire Light Infantry. He survived the war.

But another brother, the eldest, John, was killed on 17 October 1914 while serving in France with the 12th Lancers. Later, Anthony Eden's uncle, Robin Grey, commander of a squadron in the Royal Flying Corps, was shot down and captured. On 20 February 1915 Sir William died after a long illness.

Soon after his eighteenth birthday Anthony Eden volunteered for the army, like so many of his contemporaries at Eton. On 29 September he was appointed a temporary lieutenant in the 21st battalion the Yeoman Rifles, of the King's Royal Rifle Corps, a regiment dating from the eighteenth century. The newly formed Yeoman Rifles were recruited mainly from volunteer farmers and country labourers. Its first commanding officer was Lieutenant-Colonel the Earl of Feversham, a Yorkshire landowner, previously in command of the Yorkshire Hussars. Training had begun at Duncombe Park, Feversham's home, and the full establishment was reached in December. As an officer Eden impressed his subordinates more with his smart appearance and youthful good looks than ability to command. But he learned rapidly and gained in confidence. His men soon began to appreciate his easy manner and friendliness.

Early in 1916 the battalion moved south to Aldershot for intensive training. It crossed to France on 4 May as the junior battalion of the 41st division. At the end of the month it went into the line for the first time at Ploegsteert Wood. By coincidence the sector it occupied had been vacated earlier in May by the 6th Royal Scots Fusiliers, then commanded by Lieutenant-Colonel Winston Churchill. News soon reached Eden that his younger brother, Nicholas, serving as a midshipman in the Royal Navy, had been killed at the battle of Jutland. He was then only sixteen and of all the Eden children had been closest in affection to Eden. A few weeks earlier his sister's husband, Lord Brooke, the future sixth Earl of Warwick, was wounded. It seemed that every male member of his family with whom he had spent his life before the war was dead, wounded or captured.

The first phase of the war 'saw the destruction of the world as I knew it', Anthony Eden was later to write in his memoirs, *Facing the Dictators*. At the time there was no heroics in his attitude to the war raging around him, taking its toll of family, relatives and friends. Only once, when trying to comfort his mother after Nicholas' death, he wrote: 'we must all die some day, why not now by the most honourable way possible, the way that opens the gates of paradise – the soldier's death.'

The Yeoman Rifles remained in the line at Ploegsteert Wood until mid-August, attaining a high fighting reputation. In September the battalion took part for the first time in the battle of the Somme. It had been in progress since July and was to claim on both sides more than a million and a quarter casualties. A major new attack began on 15 September. Eden's battalion took part in the fierce fighting, capturing three lines of trenches near the village of Flers. The battalion suffered huge losses, including its commander, the Earl of Feversham, on 17 September. The next day Eden wrote to his mother: 'I have seen things lately that I am not likely to forget.' He asked her to make a special effort to get the wounded of his company into her care at Windlestone, which was being used as a military hospital. On 3 October Eden was appointed adjutant at the exceptionally early age of nineteen. He was the youngest person on the Western Front to hold this office – a tribute to his fine organizing talent.

On 7 October the battalion was back in the line near Flers, taking part in another attack on German trenches. After a week of constant fighting, heavy rain, and continuous shell fire, the King's Royal Rifle Corps was so savagely mauled that it ceased to exist as a Durham-recruited battalion. The ranks were now filled principally with Londoners. The rest of the year and the early part of 1917 were spent in routine trench work. On 6 May Eden and his battalion celebrated with a concert and play their first anniversary on the Western Front.

For one outstanding act of bravery Eden was awarded the Military Cross on 4 June. While entrenched at Ploegsteert in August 1916, he had been ordered to carry out a surprise raid on the German trenches. He and his men were discovered and under a hail of bullets retreated to their own lines. Eden, however, returned to the forward position to rescue the missing platoon sergeant. Although continuously fired upon, he found the wounded man and succeeded in bringing him back safely through the wire.

The Flanders campaign of 1917 opened on 7 June. Eden participated with the King's Royal Rifle Corps in the opening attack from the Ypres salient against the Messines ridge. This was the third battle of Ypres, and Eden saw action both in its opening phase and again in another advance on 31 July. On both occasions the battalion was heavily bombarded and suffered severe casualties. But the attacks were successful, and when the battalion was relieved on 4 August it was able to take up a position in the old German front line. At the end of the month the battalion was inspected by Field-Marshal Sir Douglas Haig, commander-in-chief of the British armies in France.

The last battle Eden was to participate in as a member of the Yeoman Rifles was the advance on Passchendaele. On 20 September the battalion attacked, and until the morning of the 23rd was involved in fierce trench fighting. After being withdrawn from the front lines, the King's Royal Rifle Corps spent part of October engaged in coastal defence on the Franco–Belgian border. In the middle of November the entire 41st division, including Eden's battalion, was sent to Italy, returning to France on 8 March 1918. A week later the battalion was disbanded, its officers and other ranks being distributed among various units of the regiment. Eden however had remained in France, having been promoted on 19 November 1917 from adjutant to temporary captain and general staff officer, 3rd grade, in General Sir Hubert Plummer's Second Army. It was a job he later looked back upon as 'exciting but fascinating'.

In March 1918 the last great German offensive of the war took place. Eden was stationed on the British lines near La Fère on the river Oise. Directly opposite, he was to discover much later, in 1935, was a young German corporal, Adolf Hitler. A French diplomat, hearing of this coincidence, afterwards told Eden: 'You were opposite Hitler and you missed him. You ought to have been shot.' After further promotion on 26 May Eden ended the war as a brigade major in the 198th infantry brigade.

Three years of active service on the Western Front was an experience that inevitably had a decisive effect on Eden's character. He had developed verve, assurance and self-confidence. It brought out abilities as an organizer and leader. More profoundly, he emerged, as did so many others, with a passionate detestation of war and all its suffering. In later life he was to identify himself with the 'lost generation', profoundly marked with a determination to spare future generations the horrors they had endured.

After the armistice of November 1918, Eden was tempted to stay in the army. He spent the long winter of 1918–19 with his brigade in the snows of the Ardennes. However the inanity of peacetime soldiering, occupied with army inventories and keeping his men amused, bored him. More important, he was simply discouraged by the multiplicity of generals in his regiment. On 28 March 1919 he had been transferred, still as brigade major, to the 199th infantry brigade. But his own brigadier was the thirty-ninth in succession. Eden decided to leave the army. He was demobilized on 13 June, a day after his twenty-second birthday. He relinquished his commission on completing his service and was granted the rank of captain.

So Eden returned to Windlestone Hall after four years of soldiering. Now he had to contemplate his future. After much discussion with his family, a career in the diplomatic service emerged as the favourite choice. In preparation, he decided to study oriental languages. It was not that unusual a choice if one considered, as he must have, that the languages of the Middle East would have an increasing importance and would be a great asset to a diplomatic career which might well include that area. Apparently on the advice of his mother, Eden agreed to go to Oxford, where he was accepted at Christ Church College. Having dabbled in some Turkish with a family friend after being demobilized, he decided to make Persian his main language and Arabic a secondary one.

Thus it was that Eden entered Christ Church in the autumn term of 1919 to complete an education interrupted by the war. It was an experience reflected in the unique atmosphere of Oxford at that date. The normal complement of young undergraduates was supplemented with an intake of older men who were aged beyond their years by war experiences. At first Eden found the transition from the trenches to undergraduate life alarming. With his usual capacity for hard work, he threw himself wholeheartedly into his studies. His tutor in Persian was Richard Paget Dewhurst, a former Indian judge and eastern languages scholar. Professor Margoliouth, an orientalist of world renown, was his Arabic tutor. Both treated Eden with much kindness, though their learning was sometimes beyond him. It was said of Margoliouth that he once addressed Baghdad University in such pure Arabic as to be almost unintelligible to his audience.

For four years Eden applied himself to his studies, which at that time emphasized the antique periods of oriental civilization. He had to read Darius' inscriptions at Behistun in the cuneiform in which they were cut, and Zoroastrian religious works. This was followed by the *Shâhnâme*, Persia's epic book of kings; the odes of Hâfiz; medieval braintwisting philosophic works; and of course the Koran. In later life Eden carried this learning very lightly. Winston Churchill was surprised to find this erudite stream in Eden's background when he was entertained by him, during a transatlantic flight in 1954, with long passages of Persian poetry. His studies at Oxford gave Eden an abiding interest in eastern affairs and a feeling of complete confidence when confronted with the problems of that area.

As at Eton, Eden was in no way a conspicuous Oxford undergraduate. He was a very competent scholar and obtained in 1922 a first class honours degree. But he led a rather reclusive life, barely participating in college activities. He never spoke in debates at the Oxford Union, the usual training ground for future men of public affairs. Nor did he participate in any of the university's political societies. He was, for a time, a member of the Oxford Union Dramatic Society and was president of the Asiatic Society. These were, however, only peripheral activities which in no way detracted from the course of quiet individualism he pursued.

For the most part he moved among a select group of friends with aesthetic inclinations. Prominent among them were Lord David Cecil and R. E. Gathorne-Hardy. Along with Eden, they circulated a letter in November 1920 inviting fellow students to join a small art society to be called 'The Uffizi'. It was suggested that such people as George Moore, Walter Sickert, Bernhard Berenson and Augustus John would address the society. Eden became its president, and he gave the first talk to members on the subject of Italian art from Cimabue to Tintoretto. A later paper that Eden read to 'The Uffizi' on Cézanne showed a clear-sighted appreciation of that painter far beyond its time, and owed much to Eden's father's influence. His academic routine was varied by frequent holidays abroad, especially to France and Italy, and by an active interest in the territorial army. In fact from July 1920 until May 1923 he held a commission in the 6th battalion of the Durham Light Infantry.

When he came down from Oxford in 1922 at the age of twenty-five, Eden was already a mature man. The strength of character he had developed in the war was now reinforced with a greater mental maturity. Although a slightly remote figure, he was capable of intimate friendship and generous hospitality, and had a charming and easy manner. He did, however, show that reticence of phrase which became so marked a characteristic in later years. The *bon mot* was never something that came to him easily, if at all. His whole subsequent development of personality followed lines already laid down when he left Oxford.

Eden returned to Windlestone to decide on the next stage of his career. He was now well prepared, if that was still his inclination, to enter the diplomatic service. In the end he decided against it, and instead, during the summer of 1922, he chose parliament as an alternative avenue to foreign affairs. There are few indications that he had ever before seriously contemplated this, though he is reported to have kept at Eton a map of Britain with all the safe Conservative seats plainly marked. This adolescent interest in politics had clearly lain dormant for several years. Perhaps it was the excitement attending the fall of David Lloyd George's wartime coalition government that aroused his interest in Westminster. After discussing the possibility of fighting a number of Durham seats, he was unanimously adopted as Conservative candidate for Spennymoor, then held by a Liberal. Eden had strong local connections here and it was his home ground. But the choice of the Marquess of Londonderry, a coal owner, as his principal supporter was slightly misjudged.

Eden was never a politician who enjoyed elections; he just endured them. The Spennymoor contest he always regarded as the least disagreeable in his career. During the campaign he advocated a moderate Conservatism, rooted as much in temperament as conviction. He declared himself a loyal follower of the prime minister, Andrew Bonar Law, and called for a revival of trade and a decrease in the armies of unemployed. 'The miners were pleasantly tolerant of my beliefs, though they never dreamt of voting for them', Eden later wrote. On polling day, 15 November, the seat was won by the Labour candidate, Joseph Batey, with 13,766 votes. He had gone down into the mines at the age of twelve and was at the time of the election on the executive committee of the Miners' Federation. Eden polled 7,567 votes, defeating the Liberal, while nationally the Conservatives formed the government.

The Spennymoor election had proved Eden's electoral merit. Defeat there, at one of the lowest rungs of the electoral ladder, left no adverse mark on him. Another opportunity to enter Westminster arose a year later. Sir Ernest Pollock, later Lord Hanworth, was appointed Master of the Rolls in October 1923, vacating the safe Warwick and Leamington seat. After a local candidate had dropped out, Lord Willoughby de Broke, a fellow war veteran, Military Cross holder and the party chairman, put Eden's name forward. The young lord, himself only twenty-seven, strongly defended Eden against charges of inexperience, and predicted for him a brilliant future. At his adoption meeting Eden discounted the criticisms of his detractors who said that his only recommendations were youth, good looks and good family. Instead, he emphasized his unlimited enthusiasm, his belief in the Conservative tradition and his devotion to a life of public service. He was then formally adopted to represent the Conservative party at the by-election.

The campaign was to provide more excitement for the constituency than it had known in years. For some time Eden had been engaged to Beatrice Helen Beckett, the daughter of Sir Gervase Beckett, a banker, Conservative MP for North Leeds, and chairman of the *Yorkshire Post*. On 5 November Eden broke off his campaign to go south with Miss Beckett for their elaborate marriage ceremony at St Margaret's, Westminster. After a brief two-day honeymoon in Sussex they returned to Leamington. The marriage further strengthened the existing domestic ties between Eden and his Labour opponent in the campaign – Frances, Countess of Warwick, a remarkable and beautiful woman, had embraced socialism and was fighting the seat as its first-ever Labour candidate. She was the mother-in-law of Eden's sister, Marjorie, married to the future sixth Earl of Warwick. Now Eden himself was married to the step-daughter of the Countess of Warwick's eldest daughter, Lady Marjorie Beckett, second wife of Sir Gervase. And Lady Marjorie Beckett had in fact previously been married to the Earl of Feversham, Eden's commanding officer in the war. Such extensive family connections proved invaluable to Eden's early public career.

Further interest was added to the by-election when on 16 November Stanley Baldwin, who had succeeded Andrew Bonar Law as prime minister the previous May, announced the dissolution of parliament. Baldwin decided to call a general election, claiming that he could not fight unemployment without the introduction of protection. The Warwick and Leamington campaign now became part of a national election. Polling day, 6 December, proved a disaster for the Conservative party. With only 258 MPs, they forfeited their overall parliamentary majority. For Eden, however, the Warwick and Leamington poll was a triumph. Possibly the longest electoral campaign in history gave him 16,337 votes, more than the combined total of both his Labour and Liberal opponents. Eden was destined to represent this same constituency in parliament until 1957.

Eden and his young wife took a house in Mulberry Walk, Chelsea, where they lived until 1934, when they moved to Fitzhardinge Street in Mayfair. Under the pseudonym of 'Backbencher' he started to write articles on politics for the *Yorkshire Post*, and occasionally contributed material on the arts and even gardening. The Eden marriage produced two sons, Simon Gascoign, born in 1925, and Nicholas, born in 1930 and named after his father's youngest brother.

On 5 January 1924, at the age of twenty-six, Captain R. A. Eden, as he was then called, took his oath of allegiance in the House of Commons. It was a difficult and confusing parliament that he entered. Baldwin found it impossible to govern with no overall majority. After the prime minister had been defeated on a vote of confidence, King George V called on Ramsay MacDonald on 22 January to form the first Labour government in British history.

When Eden entered parliament, as he recalled in *Facing the Dictators*, he 'knew little except war and schooling'. His mood was earnest, but on his own admission he was only sketchily informed. The young MP, among the very few new Conservative members, was advised in a private talk with Baldwin to treat the Labour government charitably, and to be neither presumptuous nor sarcastic in his speeches.

On the eve of World War II, when Eden published his first collection of speeches, *Foreign Affairs*, he chose to reprint as the opening extract his maiden speech of 19 February 1924. From the perspective of 1939 it was a sensible choice, showing how consistent his campaign for rearmament had been. But at the time it was an over-ambitious speech. He had chosen the subject of air defence for his parliamentary debut, and spoke in support of a resolution by Sir Samuel Hoare, later Lord Templewood, the previous secretary of state for air. It concerned the need for the British government to maintain a home defence air force adequate to resist aggression. After asking the Commons for the usual indulgence due to him on this occasion, Eden contended that Britain must be prepared to defend herself against attack from any quarter. He chided the opposition with being tempted to adopt the attitude of 'the terrier, and roll on their backs and wave their paws in the air with a pathetic expression. But that is not the line on which we can hope to insure this country against attack from the air.' He exhorted the government to carry out a full programme of air defence.

During his parliamentary apprenticeship, Eden formed an enormous admiration for Herbert Asquith, the former prime minister and leader of the Liberal party. He admired above all Asquith's skill at making parliamentary speeches which were models of lucidity and brevity. This is what Eden was attempting to emulate. His strengths as a speaker were to be clarity, succinctness and a mastery of detail. But he was never to become an outstanding parliamentary speaker, and it was an experience he never learned to enjoy.

In succeeding debates Eden spoke on air defence, housing, and army marriage allowances. But it was on 1 April that he made his first contribution to a debate on foreign affairs. The subject was the treaty of Peace (Turkey) bill, giving effect to certain provisions of the treaty of Lausanne, signed in July 1923 but not yet ratified. For the first time he spoke as one who could claim some first-hand knowledge of the country under discussion. His effective speech displayed a warm sympathy for the Turkish nationalism of Kemal Ataturk, and concluded with an exhortation for friendlier Anglo–Turkish relations. The speech was of further significance as it marked the beginning of Eden's parliamentary reputation as a speaker on foreign affairs. His grasp of the subject, unusual in a man of his age, combined with a pleasing manner and appearance, quickly brought him to the attention of the Commons.

The first Labour government lasted only nine months and one day. It was dissolved on 9 October 1924, and Eden was back again appealing to the electors of Warwick and Leamington. It was Ramsay MacDonald's efforts to come to better terms with bolshevik Russia and the famous episode of the Zinoviev letter which brought about the election. The results of what became known as the 'red letter' election came as no surprise. Eden easily secured re-election, increasing his majority in a campaign which saw an overwhelming swing to the Conservatives. Their parliamentary seats increased from 248 to 419, while Labour lost forty seats. The decisive losers in the campaign, however, were the Liberals, whose parliamentary representation was reduced by more than 100 members.

Stanley Baldwin began his second term as prime minister on 4 November 1924. His strong majority enabled him to govern for nearly the full parliamentary term of five years. Baldwin's personality dominated the life of this parliament, which witnessed in foreign affairs a *rapprochement* between Britain, France and Germany; and in domestic affairs, despite a coal crisis and the General Strike, a gradual improvement of economic conditions. Eden was a devout admirer of the Baldwin style of politics. Baldwin's conciliatory nature, his rejection of class distinctions, his positive statesmanship in domestic affairs and faith in the British people were qualities with which Eden easily identified. 'Baldwin was the antithesis of the hard-faced men who were alleged to have dominated the Conservative Party immediately after the first world war', Eden wrote in *Facing the Dictators*. Both in character and purpose Baldwin expressed what Eden, as a young MP with memories of British soldiers fighting together in the trenches, wished to achieve in politics at home and abroad.

Early in 1925 Eden was appointed parliamentary private secretary to Godfrey Locker-Lampson, under-secretary of state at the Home Office. The position was unpaid and required additional attendance at the House, but it was a step on the ladder of parliamentary promotion. It afforded Eden access to a government department to observe at first hand the mechanics of administration. Locker-Lampson was a cultivated former Foreign Office official, a barrister, war veteran, poet and expert on ancient Greek coins. Eden found much in common with him and gained valuable experience. The appointment was obviously due to the fact that in his first year as an MP Eden had established a network of personal relations in the House.

This first position neither taxed Eden's full resources nor proved sufficiently exacting, and he readily accepted an opportunity to travel abroad. In September 1925, through the good offices of his father-in-law, Sir Gervase Beckett, Eden was appointed to represent the *Yorkshire Post* at the Imperial Press conference in Melbourne. He travelled via Canada and across the Pacific to New Zealand and Australia, returning home after paying a brief visit to

Ceylon. The impressions he gathered appeared in a series of articles in the *Yorkshire Post* and formed the basis of a book, *Places in the Sun,* published the following year. The book was remarkable for two things, neither related to its substance. Baldwin contributed a mellifluous foreword, praising Eden's determination to see the empire at first hand. It was an unusual compliment from a prime minister to a junior MP. Secondly, the book revealed something of Eden usually hidden from public view. Among pages of comment on such topics as tariffs and immigration were passages exhibiting a keen eye for colour and beauty, a sensitive nature, and a cultivated literary style.

Returning to the House of Commons at the beginning of December, Eden's contributions to debates followed the pattern he had by now wisely chosen of speaking on subjects familiar to him. On 21 December he supported a motion put forward by Baldwin. It proposed the government's acceptance of a League of Nations Council decision affecting the northern frontiers of Iraq at Turkish expense, and called for an extension of Britain's mandate responsibility for Iraq. Eden strongly advocated the extension of the mandate within the new frontiers. Nothing would harm Britain's reputation more, he stated, than 'to scuttle, like flying curs, at the sight of our own shadow . . . our name would be a jibe in the mouth of every tavern-lounger from Marrakesh to Singapore.' In conclusion, Eden pleaded for the hand of friendship to be extended to Turkey. He sat down to cheers and the satisfaction of an impressive debating success.

Eden was adding to his growing reputation as a responsible, fair and competent speaker on foreign affairs. During March 1926 the League of Nations had failed to agree on the admission of Germany as a permanent member of the Council. It was a bitter disappointment to the foreign secretary, Sir Austen Chamberlain. The House of Commons debated the situation on 23 March. Eden was asked by the government chief whip, Bolton Eyres-Monsell, to contribute to the discussion. The best face had to be put on a difficult situation, and Eden rose brilliantly to the occasion, which had already seen such august figures as Sir Austen Chamberlain, David Lloyd George and Ramsay MacDonald contributing to the debate. Eden admitted that the League had suffered a severe rebuff. But he argued that 'to expect the League to change human nature in a year or two was an extravagant expectation'. Yet he remained optimistic, and indeed later in the year Germany was admitted to the Council of the League.

In retrospect Eden modestly commented how astonished he was to have been so rapidly 'propelled into the political stratosphere'. But it is not surprising that a chance soon arose to hold office in his chosen field of growing expertise. The competition was not keen, and distinction, which Eden possessed as opposed to brilliance, was sufficient recommendation for advancement. Besides, it was his attention to style in the form of his speeches and to detail in their substance which helped him on the road to advancement. On 28 July it was announced that he had succeeded Roger Lumley, later Earl of Scarborough, as parliamentary private secretary to Chamberlain. It was in fact Locker-Lampson, himself a former PPS to the foreign secretary, who had recommended Eden. He accepted the position with the one reservation that he be allowed to speak in the House as and when he saw fit.

To a young MP like Eden, Chamberlain presented an aloof figure, slightly forbidding in appearance and manner. However he proved a valuable mentor for Eden, just beginning a lifelong association with foreign affairs. From the foreign secretary, many years his senior, Eden imbibed the essence of traditional Foreign Office patterns of thought and conduct. He grew to accept Chamberlain's view that peace in Europe depended on stable Anglo–French relations, with both countries moving in step towards an understanding with Germany. That view, combined with Eden's deeply felt francophilism, was to become the basic structure of his pre-war outlook on international affairs. From Chamberlain he also acquired precisely those personal qualities which most distinguished the foreign secretary – tact, patience, charm in personal contacts, and competence within a rather circumscribed vision. A mutual affection developed between the two which ripened into a friendship lasting until Chamberlain's death in 1937. Chamberlain's tutelage, combined with the continuing influence of Baldwin, laid the foundation of Eden's entire personality as a public figure.

At the time of Eden's appointment as PPS, Chamberlain was still basking in the limelight of having successfully negotiated the historic Locarno treaties of December 1925. The declarations regarding the inviolability of frontiers and the mutual guarantees which they contained seemed to promise years of uninterrupted peace for Britain and the continent. The treaties had been the result of Chamberlain's patient efforts, with the help of the German and French leaders, Gustav Stresemann and Aristide Briand, to satisfy German aspirations and allay French anxieties. Within a few years Eden would be facing exactly the same dilemma in totally different circumstances.

Sir Austen Chamberlain's unremitting attendance at meetings of the League Council brought prestige to that institution. However his political instincts forced him to put a brake upon the League's idealism and upon attempts to accelerate the pace of its development. Eden missed out on his first invitation to accompany Chamberlain to Geneva. He simply could not pay, as he would have had to, his own expenses. But in September 1927 Eden was at last able to travel there and set out in a mood of curiosity and watchful interest. He took part in the ritual and pomp of the foreign secretary's journey to the continent: the top-hatted station-master and the Foreign Office representatives at Victoria, the harbourmaster at Dover bowing the party on to the ship, the *préfêt* and the mayor at Calais, the journey to Paris for dinner at the embassy, the night train from the Gare de Lyon to Geneva, and finally the arrival there at 7.30 in the morning when the whole embassy staff was paraded to meet their chief at the station. When he became foreign secretary in December 1935 Eden scrapped what he considered to be a 'barbaric' custom.

It was not the formal meetings of the Council at Geneva which impressed Eden. In the company of Chamberlain he was admitted into the private dinner conversations, and it was at such occasions that he had his first glimpses of the wit and forcefulness of Briand, and the quick, clear brain and formidable appetite of Stresemann. For someone who was in later years to be so closely identified with the League, Eden's initial impressions were reserved. He appreciated the value of Geneva as a meeting place for foreign ministers, and was struck by the efficiency of the League secretariat. More widely, the League appeared to him at the time as affording an opportunity to escape from the dangers of a balance of power approach which had failed to keep the peace, to an international authority which would have the strength to do so. He was definitely not among the fanatic League idealists. In parliament he had already declared: 'Far more harm has been done to the League by people with their heads in the clouds and their brains in their slippers than by the most inveterate enemy the League ever had.'

Throughout 1927 and the following year Eden continued to perform his parliamentary duties for Sir Austen Chamberlain with tact and an ever increasing professionalism. He had by now become an ambitious politician anxious to advance both reputation and career, though very rarely at the expense of the cheap jibe or over the backs of others. He made himself useful to others and tried to be both needed and wanted by the Conservative party. His speeches at this time show a marked tendency to avoid controversy and to smooth over difficulties. Yet they were also capable of both imagination and toughness. On 23 March 1927 Eden moved a resolution in the Commons concerning empire settlement. It was an appeal for increased emigration from Britain which was far-reaching both in its diagnosis of the causes for the low rate of emigration and in its remedies. His speech showed him to be a well-travelled, informed and forward-looking member of the House. The motion was carried without a division.

In the autumn of the following year, when Chamberlain was abroad recovering from illness, Eden had to fend for himself in the Commons. He came through with the respect of most members. In April 1929 he made another imaginative appeal to the House. Anglo–American co-operation, he told members, 'is the most important safeguard for world peace in the years that are to come'. His own premiership was to prove tragically that such a policy was not always possible. On the other hand Eden could also be tough, as when, a little later, he argued successfully that Anglo–Soviet relations, broken off in May 1927, should not be restored without previously securing the termination of anti-British propaganda. It was a similar issue during the Italian negotiations which forced him to resign in 1938.

On the eve of the general election of 30 May 1929 Eden's fundamental views on the conduct of foreign policy had been generally developed. He believed that good Anglo–French and Anglo–American relations were fundamental to the safety of Britain. He was a convinced sympathizer with the facts of national attitudes, such as French fears of war or Turkish nationalism. He was not an old-fashioned imperialist, but held that the empire was in itself a developing community for which Britain had a special responsibility. Finally, he believed that foreign policy must be conducted with patience, after very thorough preparation in the Foreign Office.

Stanley Baldwin's appeal on a slogan of 'Safety First' failed to inspire the British electorate. The Conservative majority was sharply cut from 419 to 260 seats. The Labour party, with 288 seats, began its second administration, headed again by Ramsay MacDonald. Eden had thrown himself wholeheartedly into the campaign. He thought that the Conservatives would do well, partly on the basis of an electorate swollen by the enfranchisement of women. He also thought that he would do well in his own constituency. During the six years he had represented Warwick and Leamington he had been assiduous in furthering its parliamentary interests. He made the rounds of the scattered villages of his constituency, which in those days included Stratford-upon-Avon and the surrounding district as well as Warwick, Leamington and Kenilworth. When the results were announced, however, he discovered that he had held the constituency, for what was to be the only time, on a minority vote. He polled 23,045 against his opponents' combined total of 25,326 votes.

After the Conservative party's defeat at the polls, Eden received a letter from Sir Austen Chamberlain. He wrote that Baldwin had promised that, in the event of a Conservative victory, Eden would become under-secretary at the Foreign Office. So strong did the Labour party appear in the aftermath of the election that the youthful Eden thought that such an opportunity would never return and that his political career was over.

Eden made the most of all available opportunities during the two years he spent in opposition. Early in 1930 he joined a group of young MPs which included such future Cabinet ministers as Oliver Stanley, William Ormsby-Gore, Walter Elliot and W. S. Morrison. They agreed to meet at a weekly dinner and to work together in parliament. All shared similar views, their domestic politics being to the left of centre in the Conservative party. They found that Baldwin was accessible and sympathetic to their ideas for a progressive Conservatism with their slogan of 'a property-owning democracy'.

Under the influence of this small group, Eden developed his outlook on domestic affairs to which he was to return throughout his career. In November 1929 he had told party workers in London that Conservative objectives must be 'to enable every worker to become a capitalist'. He wished to see schemes of co-partnership between industry and workers fully developed. Despite the rising tide of criticism against Baldwin from within the Conservative party, Eden for one stood solidly behind his leader, giving support both in public and in private. Eden was convinced that Baldwin alone would keep the party truly national and prevent it from becoming 'the creature of millionaire newspaper owners or a mere appanage of big business'. He was the only statesman the party possessed and its greatest electoral asset.

Ruminations on domestic affairs and defending his party leader were only one part of Eden's opposition activities. He continued to speak out frequently, with increasing authority, on foreign policy. His range of subjects widened, including the Singapore base, troubles in Palestine, Anglo–Soviet relations, India, and almost continuously the League of Nations. Coincident with the devastating economic depression which now threatened the western world, the spirit of Locarno, that eagerly-pursued era of peace and reconciliation, was beginning to fade. International affairs were again deteriorating.

Several years of preparatory work had gone into the long-awaited Disarmament conference at Geneva. In readiness for it Ramsay MacDonald had set up an all-party committee to discuss British policy. In March 1931 Eden was chosen by Baldwin, along with Sir Austen Chamberlain and Sir Samuel Hoare, to represent the Conservatives. Association with other members such as David Lloyd George, MacDonald and the Labour foreign secretary, Arthur Henderson, proved a novel and enjoyable experience for Eden. He strongly felt the overriding need, both in the national and international interest, for an arms agreement. But until agreement had been reached he remained as anxious as he had been in his maiden speech in February 1924 that Britain should be protected against her vulnerability to air attack. That was the theme of a speech he delivered in the House of Commons on 29 June 1931. Again he warned about the dangers of unilateral disarmament. 'The seeds of war psychology still exist in Europe,' he stated. The roots of conflict lay in the animosity between those nations influenced by fear and those influenced by impatience. It was essential, therefore, for Britain to build and maintain adequate air defences. Eden concluded his speech on a personal note. He vividly recalled his experience in the last war when, having stopped for the night at brigade headquarters in a farmhouse, he was subjected not to the usual barrage of shell fire but to a rain of bombs which terrorized him. 'There now, you have had your first taste of the next war', one of his companions commented.

The continued ravages of the world economic depression, coupled with severe economic difficulties in Britain, led to the resignation on 24 August of the Labour government. The following day a coalition or national government headed by MacDonald was formed to deal with the financial crisis. Baldwin became lord president of the council, and Sir Herbert Samuel, leader of the Liberal party, was appointed secretary of state for home affairs. Another Liberal, the former viceroy of India, the Marquess of Reading, took on the job of foreign secretary.

In a government that had to accommodate demands for office from three parties, Eden could have been expected to forget Baldwin's promise two years earlier of future office. Behind the scenes, however, Eden still had powerful voices recommending him. On 27 August he discovered that Sir Austen Chamberlain had urged Lord Reading to give him a Foreign Office position. Baldwin spoke likewise to MacDonald, and the following day Eden was told of this by Baldwin himself during a private conversation. He added that he regarded his young protégé as a potential prime minister in about ten years' time.

Eden was offered the position of parliamentary under-secretary of state at the Foreign Office, which he readily accepted. On 1 September he began work for the first time as a minister. Under normal circumstances the responsibilities of the under-secretary are limited. With Lord Reading in the Lords, however, Eden became the government spokesman on foreign affairs in the House of Commons. Fortunately, that subject was not at the time the major preoccupation of the national government, and during September he acted mainly as *rapporteur* to the Commons on the beginnings of the long Japanese invasion of Manchuria. The national government was completely preoccupied with trying to reorganize the nation's finances. It promptly presented an emergency budget, dissolved parliament on 7 October, and went to the country for a vote of confidence.

In the weeks prior to the election, there had been a strong current of opinion among Conservatives that the party ought to campaign unhindered by coalition obligations. Eden held out strongly against this, arguing that such a party dogfight would do irretrievable damage to the country and the economy. Only an appeal from a national government, he was convinced, would succeed. He therefore felt vindicated by the election results. Polling day, 27 October 1931, brought a sweeping victory to the national government. It emerged with 554 seats, including 473 Conservatives, which left a tiny Labour opposition of only fifty-two members, four Independent Liberals, and five others. In his own constituency, in a straight fight against a Labour candidate, Eden emerged with his largest ever majority of 29,323.

Victory at the polls again meant Cabinet changes which resulted in Eden getting a new chief. During the course of their brief association, Eden had found Reading an easy person to work with, always thoughtful and courteous. Both men in fact had a similar experience in coming to grips with work that was at once novel and trying, and both felt they were gradually mastering the job. But Reading had decided to retire gracefully, allowing MacDonald to use the vacancy to appoint Sir John Simon as foreign secretary. His reputation was then at its peak, built on his undoubted brilliance as an advocate, and fresh from his work on the Round Table conference planning the future of India. Simon's experience as an advocate was to prove his weakness as foreign secretary. It was a situation in which Eden's attractive personality, growing popularity and expertise were bound to be compared with his secretary of state. In his memoirs, *Retrospect*, Simon looked back on his appointment, confident in his skills and grateful for those on whom he could call for assistance. And among these experts he included Anthony Eden.

2

'FACING THE DICTATORS'
1932-1939

THE turbulent decade of the thirties was, among other things, a time when reputations were either made or savagely destroyed. Anthony Eden was that rare exception of a figure who made his reputation. After eight years as an MP, devoted almost exclusively to the study of foreign affairs, he had achieved position but not as yet influence. The next six years were to see him rise to foreign secretary, an internationally known, constantly photographed politician, whose personality aroused the most extreme forms of affection and antipathy.

The decade, which was to end in another world war, began with the Disarmament conference. It opened on 2 February 1932 at Geneva, under the auspices of the League of Nations. The long period of preparation unfortunately had not succeeded in solving the basic problem of how to reconcile France's need for security with Germany's demand for equality. A French plan, linking disarmament to the guarantee and coercive functions of the League might have succeeded. But it was Eden who was delegated to announce in the House of Commons that membership of the League and the existing obligations of the Locarno treaties went as far as the British government and public opinion could go in assuming commitments in Europe.

The Disarmament conference, then, was held to mark time. Eden was not a member of the British delegation, although he was well acquainted with its problems. On 17 June he told a Rhodes

Trust meeting that too much attention was being paid to the mechanics of peace and too little to its fundamentals. 'You cannot make peace by machinery', he declared; you could 'as well use a mousetrap to catch a goblin'. Efforts continued throughout the summer to meet the German claim for equality in armaments. The need for agreement grew stronger, though prospects dimmed, when in September Germany withdrew from the conference. It coincided with the beginning of Eden's active participation in the negotiations. He remained throughout a fervent believer in disarmament and a realistic negotiator. He participated in the drafting of new Foreign Office proposals which offered sufficient concessions to convince Germany in December to return to the conference.

It took another three months, however, before the British government produced a precise plan for disarmament. Eden was at the centre of this effort and instrumental in the drafting of the scheme. Early in 1933 he worked closely with Sir Alexander Cadogan, chief adviser to the British delegation at Geneva, urging an ordered pattern for the discussions. Cadogan was struck by Eden's stubborn commitment to the rights and wrongs of any issue: in the case of the former, going all out for it; in the event of the latter, being unable to be moved by 'ten million wild horses'. At the same time Eden himself began to fulfil a more seminal role when Sir John Simon, finding the work at Geneva distasteful, asked him to shoulder some of the burden.

From January to March 1933 Eden laboured incessantly. He had long conversations with his French opposite number, Pierre Cot; Lord Tyrrell, the British ambassador in Paris; Baron Aloisi, the Italian delegate to the League; and Rudolf Nadolny, the German representative. In Geneva, too, he made the acquaintance of such statesmen as Edouard Beneš of Czechoslovakia, Nicolae Titulescu, the Romanian foreign minister, and the Spaniard Salvador de Madariaga. According to the latter the League was delighted with Eden, who knew his job and impressed everyone with his efficiency, clarity and willingness to listen. On 2 March Eden secretly left Geneva with a draft copy of a disarmament convention in his possession. It was complete in all its details, specific in its proposals, and was the first plan which stood any chance of general acceptance. His obvious enthusiasm and diligence in producing such a comprehensive document had a remarkable effect in London. Ramsay MacDonald, with full Cabinet approval, agreed to present the convention to the Disarmament conference.

The task of framing proposals satisfactory to Germany had in the meantime become more difficult. For while Eden and his colleagues beavered away in Geneva and London, Adolf Hitler had been appointed German chancellor on 30 January. The strident militarism and nationalism of the Nazis, their repudiation of the pacifist policies of Gustav Stresemann, and the ominous growth of paramilitary organizations such as the SA and SS cast a dark shadow over the disarmament proceedings. On 16 March MacDonald revealed the details of the draft convention to the conference. Known as the 'MacDonald Plan', it boldly conceded to all participating states a maximum number of troops. German demands were met by stipulating that the new convention would replace the disarmament obligations of the Versailles treaty. French anxieties were allayed by a clever application of the Kellogg pact, to which the United States had been a signatory in August 1928. The British government was content that the convention entailed no new continental obligations.

Initial reactions were favourable and the conference briefly sprang to life. After adjourning for a month, it resumed and so did the disagreements and contentiousness. The momentum had disappeared, never to return again. 'One feels it is rather like a 1917 campaign in Flanders', Eden wrote to Baldwin on 1 May. 'We can only make such progress as we may in the mud between the pillboxes and leave the strong points to be attacked at the last – and as in Flanders, the pill-boxes are occupied by Germans.'

Eden remained at the centre of further desultory efforts designed to achieve the breakthrough many desired but which few believed possible. In June he participated in talks held in Paris at the instigation of the American delegate to the conference, Norman Davis. Eden then looked forward to agreement resulting from the World Economic conference about to be held in London.

The early collapse of this conference allowed only a brief discussion of disarmament questions, particularly relating to supervision and sanctions. Despite the absence of any ostensible progress, Eden remained hopeful. In the middle of September he was again in Paris in the company of Norman Davis. They found the French government, conscious of Hitler's clandestine rearmament, again concerned about security, especially during the projected period of trial disarmament. Although personally sympathetic, Eden could not convince Baldwin and Simon to offer France an increased British commitment for continental security. Compromise plans for disarmament, however, did not interest Hitler. On 14 October he announced that Germany was withdrawing from the Disarmament conference and the League of Nations.

'The Conference was becoming a sham so that it is perhaps just as well', Eden noted in his diary. On 23 October the Cabinet decided that, while maintaining the search for a reduction in armaments, Britain must increase its defence expenditure. For Hitler was at the same time demanding increased air and ground forces exceeding those specified in the Versailles treaty, and as a sop suggested a series of European non-aggression pacts. In a major speech to the League of Nations Union in Birmingham on 11 November, Eden traced the deterioration of relations in Europe to the rise of Hitler. Eden made allowances for the fact that Germany was going through a period of revolutionary change, and he maintained that British policy must continue to seek reconciliation on the continent.

Simon's handling of foreign affairs was being subjected to increasing criticism. He seemed unable to take effective decisions. The opposition attacked him relentlessly, and there were even rumblings within Conservative circles. Furthermore, Ramsay MacDonald wished to have the Foreign Office represented in the House of Lords. Just before Christmas he offered Eden the office of lord privy seal, formerly held by Baldwin. The offer elevated Eden to full ministerial rank, although he was not given a seat in the Cabinet. He was to be seconded to the Foreign Office and continue with his previous work and any assignments thought appropriate. Lord Stanhope succeeded Eden as under-secretary of state for foreign affairs, while Baldwin kept his remaining office of lord president of the council.

Eden did not in fact accept his new position until he had consulted his mentor, Stanley Baldwin. Eden was troubled by the proposed arrangement, fearing that it brought the semblance but not the reality of greater power. Baldwin reassured him on this point, hinting that the office would carry with it a privy councillorship. It was conferred six months later. He suggested to Eden that the position of lord privy seal would guarantee a strong claim for substantial advancement in the next government. Eden went to Sandringham to receive the seals of office from King George v, and on 1 January 1934 resumed his work in a new office.

The first assignment Eden undertook stemmed from the concerted attempt being made to reply to Hitler's recent rearmament and non-aggression pact proposals. The terms of the British reply, formalized in the 'Memorandum on Disarmament' of 29 January, were a compromise on the substance of the draft convention. To further prospects of its acceptance Eden was asked to visit Paris, Berlin and Rome. He was not optimistic but thought the pilgrimage worth making.

Eden and his small party of advisers were given a grand send-off from London on 16 February. In Paris a new French government, headed by Gaston Doumergue as prime minister and Louis Barthou as foreign minister, seemed wary of his mission. They voiced their suspicions of Germany's ultimate intentions, and put forward reservations regarding the British note. Eden went beyond his brief in hinting that Britain might make further commitments to ensure French security. In Berlin, on 20 February, he had his first meeting with Hitler. These were still the early days of the Nazi regime. It is not surprising, therefore, that on the whole Eden formed a relatively favourable impression of the German chancellor, regarding him as restrained, friendly, a master of his subject and amenable to negotiation. Eden discovered that his two great assets, where the Nazis were concerned, were his youth and his war experiences.

Reporting to London the details of his conversations, Eden overflowed with optimism. Hitler had made only moderate demands pertaining to defensive weapons and now agreed to supervision during a probationary period of disarmament. He promised to curb the paramilitary organizations, although he ruled out Germany's return to the League. Eden confidently looked forward to the signature of a supervised arms agreement. He was so committed to this project that he was willing to see any agreement signed rather than have nothing to show after two years' work. As a relief from the tension of these negotiations, he took refuge for an afternoon in the Kaiser-Friedrich Museum, and spent a short time with the legendary German president, Field-Marshal Paul von Hindenburg.

On arrival in Rome, Eden found telegrams awaiting him which

showed that his optimism was not shared in London. In fact, confidence in his handling of the tour was being eroded. On 26 February he met for the first time the Italian prime minister, Benito Mussolini. The duce was at his best and impressed Eden with his vigorous and entertaining personality, and his 'journalist's inquisitiveness' for foreign news. The pace of German rearmament worried him and he counselled Eden to accept Hitler's terms. The talks proceeded so smoothly that Eden decided to cut short his stay and return to Paris as he had previously arranged. There he made no further progress. He was disappointed to discover that the French Cabinet had not even discussed the 'Memorandum on Disarmament'.

On 1 March Eden returned to London, disappointed and virtually empty-handed. The opportunity to circumscribe Germany with a freely negotiated agreement had in his view been lost. He had always been sympathetic to France's demands for security. The British government had felt unable to satisfy them. After giving the House of Commons an account of his journey on 14 March, Eden ended with the blunt warning that without agreement the country would have to fall back on a desperate arms race. He had really fought a losing battle. Most Cabinet ministers already regarded disarmament as a failure. The decisive choice between modifying the 'Memorandum' or plunging ahead with rearmament was made in Paris. On 17 April the French government, alarmed by the increases announced in Germany's defence estimates, declared that all possibility of disarmament negotiations had been destroyed and that henceforth France must concentrate on strengthening her security.

The Disarmament conference met on 29 May for what was to be its last session. The French foreign minister, Louis Barthou, attacked the Germans and criticized the British. Simon contented himself with platitudes about the continued need for a convention. A complete breakdown was avoided, but for practical purposes disarmament and the Disarmament conference were dead. Eden tried at the time to disguise his deep disappointment. In a broadcast talk from Geneva, he argued that there were no cast-iron guarantees for security which could enable France to condone Germany's rearmament, without which Hitler would not sign any convention.

Eden had given his best over a period of two years to the search for disarmament. That had failed, but it had made his reputation and enriched his experiences as a politician and diplomat. He was enough of a realist to begin examining alternatives with equal application. In a speech to his constituents at Kenilworth on 28 June, he dismissed unilateral disarmament as the height of folly. Instead, he put the influence he had now achieved behind a policy which, while supporting the League of Nations, emphasized Britain's defensive needs in a period of growing international tension. His views reflected the debate about future military strategy then preoccupying all branches of the British government. The issues involved were the conflicting strategic demands of the Far East and Europe, and the extent of Britain's military commitments on the continent. The results of this debate, which Eden made a special point of defending, were the decision to add forty-four squadrons to the Royal Air Force and Baldwin's historic declaration that Britain's frontier was no longer the chalk cliffs of Dover but the banks of the Rhine.

Although increasingly at the centre of political affairs now, Eden had never forgotten the advice given him long ago by Sir Austen Chamberlain: 'You must have something else to think about or you won't sleep.' Eden had tried not to forget this. At every opportunity, rare as they were, he would indulge in his favourite pastimes, painting and art appreciation. This provided an escape for him from the frantic world of politics and diplomacy which he thoroughly enjoyed but which was soon to exact its own price. His interests were well known and in the following year were to receive official recognition. Ramsay MacDonald recommended Eden as his replacement for the seven-year term of office as a Trustee of the National Gallery. Eden delightedly accepted and served in fact two terms, forming in that time a close friendship with the director, Kenneth Clark.

Early in October Eden found some relief from his diplomatic preoccupations in a goodwill tour he made to Sweden, Denmark and Norway. He found it useful to exchange political views and describe to interested hosts his work on disarmament and his conversations with Hitler and Mussolini. Europe, however, was by this time in the throes of a crisis which evoked memories of the murder at Sarajevo in 1914. On 9 October King Alexander of Yugoslavia, while on a state visit to France, was assassinated along with Barthou by a Macedonian terrorist. Italy and Hungary were suspected of complicity, for both countries wished to foment trouble in Yugoslavia. The Balkans seemed once again on the verge of war. In response to a Yugoslav appeal at the end of November, the League decided to appoint a *rapporteur* to mediate in the crisis. Britain was well placed to exercise a restraining influence, and Eden's initial remarks to the Council had been commended for their tactfulness. After considerable prompting, he accepted the invitation to act as *rapporteur*. It was his first critical international responsibility, and one of the most difficult assignments of his career.

Eden worked quickly and methodically at formulating a compromise resolution for the League Council. Behind the scenes he held intensive private meetings with the principal officials concerned. His aim was to satisfy Yugoslavia's demands for retribution without imposing unnecessary humiliation on the Hungarians. In a dramatic meeting of the Council, at midnight on 10 December, the terms of the resolution which he had framed were revealed. They censured 'certain Hungarian authorities' for negligence relating to acts connected with the murders. Hungary was asked to investigate and report its findings to the League. The Council was invited to study the question of terrorism and draft a convention on its suppression. The proposals were unanimously accepted. The general relief expressed the next day testified to the diplomatic skill Eden had displayed, and enormously enhanced his prestige in international circles.

The future status of the Saar was another problem which had preoccupied the League at the time, and in which Eden was to play a vital role. As compensation for German wartime damage the Versailles treaty had ceded the Saar coalmines to France and placed the entire area along the basin of the river Saar under the rule of a League commission for fifteen years. In January 1935 the Saarlanders were to vote either for returning to Germany, becoming French, or preserving the status quo. The League had already organized the technical problems of the plebiscite, and it very much wanted its first such experience to be successful. For several months, however, the Nazis had been carrying out a campaign of terror and intimidation in the Saar. To ensure public order during the elections, Eden became convinced that international military supervision would be necessary. It proved to be Baldwin who overcame Cabinet reluctance to his proposal for the participation of British troops. Eden ignored some last-minute misgivings by the Cabinet, and on 5 December he announced his proposals to the Council. With French and German agreement, troops from Britain, Italy, Sweden and the Netherlands arrived in the Saar by Christmas. Under their watchful eye the peaceful elections on 13 January produced a ninety per cent vote in favour of reunion with Germany. The elections had been a success for an important experiment in international co-operation, and another display of Eden's negotiating skills. For the meantime relief predominated over any anxiety that Hitler's Reich had regained its first former German territory.

Early in 1935 several high-level meetings were held between the great powers, and a series of agreements were concluded which changed the diplomatic map of Europe. The French government began by mending its relations with the Italians, at a price to be exacted later in Africa, in an agreement signed on 7 January. At the end of the month Eden joined MacDonald, Simon and Baldwin in talks with the new French prime minister, Pierre Etienne Flandin, and his foreign secretary, Pierre Laval. It was the first time that Eden had ever represented the British government at an international conference in London. Three days of conversations resulted in an agreement to attempt a general settlement with Germany. A communiqué issued on 3 February proposed the conclusion of mutual assistance pacts in eastern Europe, an arms agreement with Germany to replace the restrictions of the Versailles treaty, an air pact to supplement the Locarno treaties, and Germany's return to the League. Hitler replied by inviting British representatives to Berlin for further discussions. At the same time the Soviet government asked for consultations in Moscow. It was decided on 4 March that Simon and Eden would go to Berlin, but Eden alone would visit eastern Europe.

On 5 March Hitler unexpectedly postponed the visit in protest against the increases in British defence estimates announced the previous day. On 9 March worse news followed from Berlin. It was revealed that Germany already possessed an air force. A week later Hitler declared that he intended to reintroduce conscription and build a peacetime army of thirty-six divisions, about 550,000 troops – all in contravention of the Versailles treaty. On 18 March the Cabinet decided to lodge a stiff protest against this illegal action, and at the same time proposed going ahead with the visit, which Hitler readily accepted. It was felt in London that something could be salvaged from the disappointing turn of events.

Simon and Eden spent 25 and 26 March in Berlin talking to Hitler and other members of the German government. Hitler objected to the proposed eastern Locarno pact. He refused to give any assurances on the independence of Austria, or of Germany's return to the League. He also lodged a fresh claim for the return of Germany's former colonies. While discussing the question of arms limitation, Hitler made the startling assertion, untrue in fact, that Germany's air strength had reached parity with Britain's. 'There was no triumph in his tone, but there was grim foreboding in my heart', Eden wrote in *Facing the Dictators*. Reflecting on what was to be his last meeting with Hitler, he decided that there was no possibility for a settlement with Hitler. This conclusion was based as much on Hitler's negative attitude as on the noticeable change in his demeanour and tone since their previous meeting.

As his train approached the Soviet Union, Eden was excited and curious. His contacts at Geneva with the Soviet foreign minister, Maxim Litvinov, had always been friendly. Indeed, Eden had warmly welcomed the decision of the USSR to join the League in September 1934. Personally he seemed free of the ideological antipathy towards bolshevism displayed by many of his ministerial colleagues. On the morning of 28 March Eden arrived in Moscow. Under the impact of his disappointing talks with Hitler, he was very frank and forthcoming with the Russians, who in turn reciprocated. The highlight of his visit was the unique experience of a personal meeting with Joseph Stalin, the secretary of the communist party. It was the first time that he had received a political representative from the west. Moreover, Eden was the first British minister to visit the Soviet Union since the bolshevik revolution. He was, and remained for years afterwards, impressed by Stalin's natural good manners, pragmatism and quality of mind. Eden was nonetheless aware that Europe's 'quietest dictator' was among the most ruthless. Stalin spoke about the dangers to European peace posed by Nazi Germany and favoured a scheme of security pacts. In reply to criticism, Eden maintained that British foreign policy was neither vacillating nor sinister, but tended to be hesitant, having to take into account world-wide interests.

A round of social functions interspersed the political discussions. There were official banquets, meetings with top Soviet commissars, and visits to the opera house. Eden was given a rare glimpse of the Soviet collection of French impressionist and post-impressionist paintings, and some early work by Picasso, still denigrated in the USSR as 'bourgeois art'. Finally, there was a luncheon at Litvinov's country *dacha*, with the table graced by a centrepiece of butter inscribed with the slogan 'Peace is Indivisible'. The official communiqué marking the end of the visit summed up the desire expressed by both sides to ensure European security as originally set out in the Anglo–French communiqué of 3 February. Although Eden had achieved nothing concrete in Moscow, the ground had been broken upon which something could be built if the European situation demanded Anglo–Soviet collaboration.

The next stop in Eden's itinerary was Warsaw, where he arrived on 1 April. He spoke to Colonel Jozef Beck, the foreign minister, and to the aging and inarticulate president, Marshal Jozef Pilsudski. Eden was told in very strong terms by both statesmen that Poland would have nothing to do with any eastern European pact. She preferred to deal separately with her giant neighbours. In Prague Eden was once again among sympathetic colleagues. It was no surprise to hear from Beneš that Czechoslovakia favoured the projected regional arrangements.

On his homeward-bound flight Eden's plane flew into a snow-storm. He and the other passengers were buffeted and bruised. After a forced landing at Cologne and an examination by a German doctor Eden was given the alarming news that his heart had been severely strained. Further examination by doctors in London, including King George V's own heart specialist, confirmed Eden's worst fears. He would need six weeks to recover. Another cause for dismay was that he could not now join, as previously arranged, the British delegation preparing for the Stresa conference with France and Italy.

Eden had anticipated appearing before the Cabinet to report on his trip. Instead, he forwarded a written report. Britain must continue to support the League and the collective peace system, he wrote, and not be intimidated by Germany's growing demands. In practical terms he advocated a series of mutual assistance pacts combined with a general non-aggression treaty open to all interested powers. Opinion in the Foreign Office supported these views. But the Cabinet was too divided to take its lead from a still youthful minister.

Eden spent a fortnight at home in London regaining his strength. He continued his recovery, accompanied by his family, at a cottage in Kent lent by the chairman of *The Times*, Major John Astor, and then with the art patron and fellow MP, Sir Philip Sassoon, at Trent Park. These were days of leisure which the Edens thoroughly enjoyed. Anthony Eden's political career was already involving him in prolonged absence from the enjoyment of normal family life. His wife Beatrice had always taken a lively interest in his political work and helped him in numerous ways, but she had a more relaxed attitude than he to the whole political world. Her interests were predominantly social and artistic, and she was a painter in her own right. Together the Edens shared this interest and a liking for the less serious cinema. The seeds of marital discord, when Mrs Eden was to declare that politics frankly bored her, still lay in the future.

It was from Trent Park, in the meantime, that Eden in early April followed developments at the Stresa conference. What reply were Britain, France and Italy to give Hitler, and what was to be the future shape of European security? Eden had urged one course of action. Others still hoped Germany would return to the League and play her part as a peaceful European neighbour. The Stresa conference gave the appearance but lacked the substance of a united front against Germany. The proposal for eastern European pacts was reaffirmed, and the conference condemned Germany's repudiation of the disarmament clauses of the Versailles treaty. Shortly afterwards France revealed her true apprehension of Germany by signing on 2 May a mutual assistance pact with the Soviet Union.

By the middle of May Eden was sufficiently recovered to return to work. In his absence, mounting pressure for a reconstruction of the national government had led to open discussion of possible Cabinet changes. Eden's name was among those mentioned for the Foreign Office. He was prepared to accept the fact that he might be too young to become foreign secretary. He was not ready, however, to serve again as lord privy seal. The reason for this rigid attitude, as he explained to Baldwin, was that he had come to certain conclusions about foreign policy which made it necessary for him either to enter the Cabinet or propagate his views from the backbenches. Baldwin, who was about to become prime minister for the third time, decided on a compromise. He had to balance

Eden's claim to the Foreign Office, for which there was much government and popular support, against objections by others and the strong claim by Sir Samuel Hoare, secretary of state for India and Burma. Eden was asked therefore to share power with Hoare and was given the Cabinet post of minister without portfolio for League of Nations affairs. Unfortunately, Hoare could get no help from Baldwin as to the details of power-sharing other than the directive 'to settle direct with the young man'. Eden admitted in retrospect that the compromise was a mistake. Only his loyalty to Baldwin prevented a row at the time. Moreover, he did not yet have the confidence to resist the pressure of his seniors. Reluctantly he accepted this new and anomalous position. His appointment was announced on 7 June, the same day that Baldwin became prime minister by exchanging positions with MacDonald.

Baldwin's appointment of a League of Nations minister co-incided with the gravest crisis yet faced at Geneva. On 5 December 1934 an incident had occurred at the Abyssinian oasis of Wal Wal near the Italian Somaliland frontier. It proved to be the opening shot in Mussolini's campaign to enhance his state with its first Fascist colony. On 3 January 1935 Emperor Haile Selassie had brought the issue to the attention of the League and asked for measures to be taken to safeguard peace. From the earliest stages of the dispute, Eden was filled with foreboding as to Italy's ultimate intentions, writing to Hoare on 23 February: 'It is hard to believe that Italian ambitions are limited to a few wells.' Eden adopted the view that a hard line must be taken with Italy and that Mussolini must be clearly warned by Britain and France about the consequences of military action.

The developing crisis posed a threat to the fragile display of Anglo–French–Italian unity established at the Stresa conference. It was essential not to alienate Mussolini if he was to be prevented from moving closer to Hitler, and if he was to continue, as previously, to help maintain the independence of Austria. Italian friendship was equally important to preserve peace in the Mediterranean, the vital British supply route to the Far East. Finally, the French government was determined not to estrange its southern neighbour. In fact in January the French foreign minister, Pierre Laval, had secretly given Mussolini a free hand in Abyssinia in exchange for close co-operation in Europe against Germany. In the following months the issue was decided as to whether Italian friendship was worth more than Abyssinian independence, and whether national interest was to prevail over international law as embodied in the League of Nations.

Eden was now at the centre of decision-making on the Abyssinian crisis. On 25 May he had already achieved another of his notable successes. He had persuaded the Italians at Geneva to agree to a resolution acknowledging the right of the Council to institute arbitration proceedings. Both parties in the dispute agreed meanwhile not to resort to force. But Eden's policy of strong action against Italy through the League was opposed by more cautious Cabinet ministers who wished to preserve Italian friendship at almost any cost. In the middle of June Eden was delegated to visit Mussolini with a plan intended to buy off Italy. It offered to a landlocked Abyssinia access to the sea on the British Somali coast in exchange for territorial concessions to Italy in the Ogaden in the south of the country.

Eden's outward journey was broken by a stopover in Paris made necessary by the signature of the Anglo–German naval agreement on 18 June. This agreement had limited the Germany navy to thirty-five per cent of British strength and conceded her right to a submarine force equal to that of the British empire. The French government had been outraged by this unilateral act of Anglo–German diplomacy. Eden was given the thankless task of mending relations with the French. In this he succeeded, and then continued to Rome, where on 24 and 25 June he discussed the British deal with Mussolini. The talks were a disaster. Mussolini contemptuously rejected the proposals and declared that he was determined to settle the Abyssinian question even to the point of risking war. In *Facing the Dictators* Eden tried to dispute accounts current at the time regarding the stormy nature of his two conversations, alleging that they were friendly. Whatever the truth, there is no doubt that he returned to London with a marked personal detestation of Mussolini. It was an attitude reciprocated by Italian propaganda, for whom Eden soon became the principal villain among western statesmen.

Reporting to the Cabinet on 3 July Eden stated that his meeting had removed any doubts as to Mussolini's belligerent intentions. There seemed little alternative but to persevere with a dual policy which Hoare described as negotiations with Italy and respect for the collective obligations of the League covenant based on continued Anglo-French co-operation. Eden supported the latter part of that dual policy, for, as he told the Cabinet, upon it lay the whole post-war system of alliances and security agreements in Europe. However, Hoare was beginning to place increasing emphasis on negotiations with Italy, with ultimately disastrous results.

The League arbitrators appointed to resolve the Abyssinian dispute made no progress. In early August Eden attended a meeting in Paris with French and Italian representatives to try and moderate Mussolini's demands. Afterwards Eden telegraphed to London that negotiations had finally broken down and that reinforcements should be sent to the Mediterranean. He believed that the time to deter Mussolini had passed. The Cabinet, however, was still divided between upholding the League or losing an ally. On 22 August it concluded that Britain must keep in step with France and, when necessary, follow the covenant procedures for dealing with an aggressor state.

In a speech to the opening meeting of the Council on 4 September, Eden warned that the crisis threatened the very survival of the League. The Council appointed a Committee of Five, including Eden and Laval, to examine the larger issue of Italo–Abyssinian relations. Sir Samuel Hoare, although in poor health, arrived on 9 September in Geneva, where he had three important conversations with Laval. They broadly agreed that in the event of war with Italy there would have to be a most cautious approach to the imposition of sanctions and certainly no rushing into any extreme measures. On 11 September Hoare publicized that part of his policy which involved trying to bluff Mussolini by a display of loyalty to the League. He delivered a stirring and universally acclaimed speech to the assembly which gave new confidence to member states. He reaffirmed Britain's determination to abide by the covenant and participate in the 'steady and collective resistance to all acts of unprovoked aggression'.

Mussolini was unimpressed by Hoare, rejected the report of the Committee of Five and proceeded with his plans to invade Abyssinia. Eden continued to send stiff telegrams to London, urging that there should be no wavering from Hoare's declaration at Geneva. In the early hours of 3 October Italian troops and mechanized forces attacked Abyssinia. The Council endorsed the conclusions of a committee, inspired by Eden, that Italy had resorted to war in violation of its obligations to the covenant. For the first time in its history the League of Nations had to apply sanctions.

In the following weeks Eden emerged at Geneva as the principal driving force in the implementation of sanctions. He was the leading figure in the Committee of Eighteen, or Sanctions Committee, remorselessly pushing through a series of measures designed to make sanctions bite. The speed and incisiveness of his work in denying to Italy arms and raw materials rankled isolationist opinion in Britain and aroused Cabinet criticism. Hoare cautioned him to go as slowly as possible and keep in step with the French.

Interest moved from Geneva to London when on 23 October Baldwin announced a general election. He campaigned on a platform of firm support for the League and modest rearmament. Eden proved to be one of the government's major election assets, epitomizing all that was best in the national government's foreign policy. His constituency honoured him with the freedom of Leamington. His campaign speeches centred on the theme that the League offered the only means to avoid another world war. On polling day, 14 November, he was given an overwhelming majority of 24,816 votes. The national government rode to an easy victory, with its seats reduced, but still with a considerable majority.

Eden returned to Geneva where the sensitive question of oil had at last been scheduled for discussion by the Sanctions Committee. The French considered it as equivalent to a declaration of war. Hoare was convinced that it would have irrevocably closed the door to further negotiations. Eden, however, regarded it as the one measure which would give sanctions credibility, nor did he fear that it would goad Mussolini into 'a mad-dog act'. Furthermore, he believed that a display of the League's effectiveness would act as a future deterrent to Germany. On 2 December the Cabinet agreed to impose oil sanctions but to delay its implementation while peace efforts continued. In 1938 Mussolini confided to Hitler that this one sanction would have crippled his entire campaign in Abyssinia.

While the momentum of sanctions had gathered speed, the Cabinet had on 23 October given Hoare authority to explore in Paris the possibilities for a negotiated settlement. He was single-mindedly dedicated to bring the fighting in Abyssinia to an end not at the League but at the conference table. In the course of two conversations with Laval, on 7 and 8 December, Hoare initialled a definitive peace plan. It involved the outright concession to Italy of about two-thirds of Abyssinia and a virtual protectorate over the remainder, which was to have an outlet to the sea. Details of this 'Hoare–Laval pact' were leaked to the French press. The ensuing public outcry and indignant charges that an aggressor state should have been rewarded were to lead to Hoare's resignation.

Loyalty to a colleague and the desire to know Hoare's motives prompted Eden to reject resignation in a situation clearly embarrassing to himself. On his insistence, the Cabinet agreed on 9 December to communicate the peace plan to Addis Ababa at the same time as to Rome. He then persuaded ministers to approve a speech he wished to make at Geneva. It amounted to a death-warrant for the Hoare–Laval pact. Only such a course, Eden argued, could dispel the League impression that Hoare's speech of 11 September, his own work on the Sanctions Committee, and the pledges of the general election had not been abandoned.

Eden delivered his speech to the League Council on 18 December. The same day Hoare submitted his resignation as foreign secretary. His dual policy of upholding the League and conciliating Mussolini was in ruins. Baldwin now offered Eden the post of foreign secretary. Having been so disappointed in June, Eden replied that the job had little attraction in the middle of a major crisis. 'It looks as if it will have to be you', was Baldwin's peremptory retort. On 22 December Eden became foreign secretary, at the age of thirty-eight, the youngest holder of the office since Lord Greville's appointment in 1791. Although disliked by several senior Cabinet colleagues, Eden's appointment was nationally a popular choice. It demonstrated Baldwin's fidelity to the League and helped restore the standing of his government.

Eden succeeded to what he called 'a wretchedly disorganised heritage'. It was more than ever unlikely that Mussolini would be amenable to a peaceful settlement of the Abyssinian dispute. Anglo–French relations were strained, and the prestige of the League had received a shattering blow. In the aftermath of the Hoare–Laval plan, the Cabinet decided on 26 February 1936 to implement oil sanctions against Italy, providing other concerned League powers acted similarly. Baldwin considered this vital for internal political reasons. Neither he nor Eden had any illusions that without American co-operation this sanction would prove ineffective.

The problem of Germany had begun meanwhile to occupy as

much of Eden's attention as the Abyssinian war. Among his first acts as foreign minister was to circulate a Cabinet paper illustrating what he regarded as Hitler's conscious aim to dominate the continent. The suggestion was made that Britain must adopt a policy of appeasement through strength. Concessions to Germany were to be extended only as part of a general European settlement which must include arms limitation and Germany's return to the League. Before Eden had a chance to work out the details of this policy, which was neither original nor without its dangers, Hitler suddenly acted. He calculated that with the League in disarray, with Italy preoccupied in Abyssinia, and with Anglo–French relations at a low point, reaction would be stifled. On 7 March German troops reoccupied the Rhineland – the demilitarized zone established by the Versailles treaty to provide security for France, and guaranteed against aggression by the Locarno treaties of 1925. In a clever display of the stick and carrot approach, Hitler coupled his breach of the Versailles and Locarno treaties with an offer to conclude non-aggression pacts and rejoin the League.

Eden now faced the first test of his judgment and abilities as foreign secretary. His responsibility was enhanced in view of Baldwin's relative indifference to foreign policy issues. Eden was to find the exercise of power more complex than the perspective suggested as a backbencher or junior minister. He was to discover that compromise and moderation had to accompany the exercise of power.

Eden admitted in *Facing the Dictators* that 'academically speaking' force should have been used, if necessary, to stop Hitler's first breach of an accepted international obligation. At the time, however, he had convinced himself that France would not resist the remilitarization of the Rhineland. He was aware of growing pro-German sentiment among sections of the British public who were content to see Germany reoccupy its 'own back garden'. Consequently the objectives Eden set for himself at the outset of the crisis were to avert war, create conditions for negotiations, and to succeed in those negotiations.

On 9 March Eden referred to one of his most basic beliefs when he told the Cabinet that Hitler 'had struck a severe blow at that principle of the sanctity of treaties which underlies the whole structure of international relations'. That statement was for the record. He advised the Cabinet, which approved, that Germany should be condemned for her breach of a treaty freely negotiated and voluntarily signed. The League should meet to discuss the situation, but sanctions were out of the question. Finally, he suggested that they now had an opportunity to conclude a far-reaching settlement with Germany. After attending a meeting in Paris of the remaining Locarno powers – France, Italy and Belgium – Eden held out to the Cabinet, on his return on 11 March, some hope for a policy of negotiation.

In the following week the Locarno powers gathered in London for discussions, and the League Council held several meetings in St James's Palace. The results of the extensive consultations were made known on 19 March. The League Council condemned Germany's action and made no mention of sanctions. The Locarno powers reaffirmed their obligations, which were now to be reinforced by Anglo–French–Belgian staff talks. In exchange for Hitler not increasing his forces in the Rhineland, Britain, France and Belgium promised to negotiate on Hitler's latest offer and summon a world security conference. Explaining his policy to the House of Commons on 26 March, Eden ambitiously committed himself to a settlement aimed at 'the appeasement of Europe as a whole'. His speech was among the best that he had ever made in the Commons, and the vote went in favour of the government.

Considering British unpreparedness to fight Hitler, French reluctance to react with force, and the steps he had initiated for new negotiations with Germany, Eden had successfully defused a dangerous situation. But the criteria for judging his approach lay in its success, and that depended on Hitler's co-operation. His initial response did not satisfy Eden, who felt it imperative to get a definite statement of Germany's final claims and aims. After submitting such a questionnaire to the Cabinet, which weakened much of its point, the document was submitted to Hitler in early May. On the 14th he made it clear that he had no intention as yet to reply, and in fact he never did. If Eden had any regrets at the failure of the secondary objectives of his Rhineland diplomacy, he never made them known. A settlement with Germany was to elude both him and his successor.

The Rhineland crisis had only temporarily diverted attention from the war in Abyssinia. Military operations intensified with the Italians advancing on the capital, their progress speeded by air supremacy and the use of poison gas. The question of oil sanctions was hardly raised, the time for its application having passed. On 2 May Emperor Haile Selassie left Addis Ababa. A week later Mussolini announced the succession of the King of Italy as emperor to the vacant throne.

At Geneva on 20 April, Eden had called for a continuation of existing sanctions, hoping they could be used as a bargaining counter with the Italians and as a moral gesture to cloak the obvious disgrace of the League. But the sanctions front was rapidly weakening, especially in the Cabinet. It was split wide open by Neville Chamberlain, the chancellor of the exchequer. Without consulting Eden, and in a deliberate attempt to give a lead to the country, Chamberlain on 10 June described the continuation of sanctions as 'the very midsummer of madness'. This statement effectively pronounced the end of League resistance to Mussolini. Eden realized that his approach to the problem had been undermined. Only Chamberlain's personal apology prevented him from resigning. The Cabinet decided on 17 June to take the initiative at the League in raising sanctions. It was naturally a blow to Eden's prestige, but also an honest and dignified decision avoiding the danger of sanctions just petering out. In early July the League Assembly agreed that sanctions should end on the 15th.

The League of Nations had been instrumental in helping Eden to achieve prominence. His fundamental political faith had been rooted in the conviction that peace depended on member states making it an effective international force. With British foreign policy having suffered so much during the Abyssinian crisis, Eden turned his mind towards reforming the League. Unfortunately, three days after sanctions against Italy were lifted, a military revolt broke out in Spain against the recently elected popular front government. Within days Spain was enveloped in a civil war that was to end only in March 1939. Within weeks the war threatened the precarious stability of Europe, with Germany and Italy materially supporting the Nationalists, led by General Francisco Franco, and the USSR committed to the cause of the republican Loyalists. As the tensions of Europe were acted out on the Spanish stage, the conflict threatened to spread to the rest of the continent.

'I told Eden yesterday that on no account, French or other, must he bring us in to fight on the side of the Russians', Baldwin remarked on 27 July. Rarely, if ever, had he given Eden so forceful a directive. But having done so, the prime minister took no further interest in Spain and was soon abroad recovering from ill-health. The formulation of British policy was left to Eden, whose single aim became to localize the Spanish civil war and restrain other powers from influencing its outcome. He was fortunately helped by the newly elected French prime minister, Léon Blum. Eden took an instant liking to this cultivated French socialist, a friendship which grew over the years. They shared a mutual interest in rare books and good literature. They also shared the conviction that Anglo–French solidarity was crucial in the uncertain state of Europe. Although sympathetic, like Eden, to the Loyalists, Blum responded to his own Cabinet pressure to issue on 2 August an invitation to interested powers to join in a Non-Intervention agreement. Eden positively welcomed this suggestion, and by the end of the month Britain, France, Italy, Germany and the USSR had agreed on non-intervention and banned the export of war materials to Spain.

This was followed by another French initiative, readily accepted by Eden, to supervise the details of non-intervention and investigate breaches of the agreement. The Non-Intervention Committee met for the first time in London on 9 September. Within a month the proceedings had degenerated into a habitual routine of polemics and contentiousness. Germany, Italy and the USSR vigorously denied violating the agreement, while stepping up their flow of war material to Spain. As infractions increased, parliamentary unity in support of non-intervention broke down. On 29 October Eden defended government policy in the Commons. He described non-intervention as 'an improvised safety curtain' designed to limit the risks of a general war. Baldwin supported this view by arguing that it was better to have a leaky dam than no dam at all.

A welcome boost to Eden's tarnished prestige had been provided meanwhile by events in the eastern Mediterranean. Previous attempts to put Britain's relations with its former protectorate of Egypt on a permanent footing had run into difficulties. The Abyssinian war, as well as the massing of Italian troops in Libya, had alarmed the Egyptian government. Eden therefore concentrated his attention on the main problem, which was the future defence of Egypt. Tactful concessions by both sides enabled agreement to be reached by 26 August. The Anglo-Egyptian treaty made provision for Egyptian independence, transferred all British troops to the Suez canal zone, and allowed Egyptian civilians, officials and troops to return to the Sudan. The treaty was to survive as the cornerstone of Britain's Middle East defence structure for eighteen years of its twenty-year term. It was also the beginning of Eden's long and fatal involvement with Egyptian affairs.

On 20 November Eden delivered a major speech to his constituents in Leamington. The theme of his remarks, like others he made at the time, was that Britain must be militarily strong if its ideals were to prevail in a rearming world. He emphasized that British arms would only be used in self-defence, in defence of the empire, and in fulfilment of specific treaty obligations. If a European settlement was reached, he added, they would even be used to defend Germany. Significantly, he insisted that the country had no automatic obligation under the League covenant to help a victim of aggression. The speech was to remain the fundamental statement on the subject for the next three years.

For several months Eden had been resisting pressure to come to an agreement with Mussolini. A timely concession, it was argued in the Cabinet, would be reciprocated to the benefit of both Britain and France. But it was the strategic argument of the chiefs of staff, anxious to pacify the Mediterranean, which finally convinced Eden. Some soothing words from Mussolini on 1 November paved the way to a lowering of the temperature between London and Rome. The same speech had in fact announced the birth of the Rome-Berlin Axis, a product of the diplomatic tensions of the Abyssinian war and Italian–German co-operation in Spain. On 2 January 1937 the Anglo–Italian 'gentlemen's agreement' was signed. It comprised an exchange of assurances, disclaiming any desire by the two signatories to modify the status quo in the Mediterranean area. Within days the Foreign Office received further reports of Italian troops arriving in Spain, in clear violation of the spirit of the agreement.

On 7 January Eden circulated in the Foreign Office a memorandum outlining his views on the wider implications of the Spanish conflict. If the Nazi-fascist adventure in Spain was not checked, he argued, Europe's future danger spots – Memel, Danzig and Czechoslovakia – would be threatened. 'It follows that to be firm in Spain is to gain time, and to gain time is what we want.' He therefore made the drastic proposal that the Royal Navy be used to supervise the entry of shipping into Spanish ports, and that it be given the rights of search. The scheme failed to get ministerial approval. It was decided to make existing non-intervention control schemes more effective. By the middle of March a limited system of supervision at Spanish ports had been grudgingly accepted. But the dam continued to leak. Adding insult to injury, Franco began his own blockade of the Spanish coast. Only a stiff warning from Eden in April prevented British shipping from being halted on the high seas. It was a small measure of success for Eden in a period of bitter disappointment and frustration.

Having weathered the abdication crisis of Edward VIII in December 1936, Baldwin looked forward to retiring after the coronation of King George VI. On 28 May 1937 the office of prime minister was handed over to Baldwin's 'crown prince', Neville Chamberlain. Simon became chancellor of the exchequer; Hoare, who had returned to the Cabinet in June 1936 against Eden's objections, went to the Home Office; and Lord Halifax, former lord privy seal, became lord president of the council. They were to constitute Chamberlain's 'inner Cabinet'. By temperament, age and outlook Eden found himself more sympathetic with younger ministers such as Duff Cooper, first lord of the Admiralty, Lord De La Warr, lord privy seal, Walter Elliot, secretary of state for Scotland, and Oliver Stanley, president of the Board of Trade.

Chamberlain and Eden had always been close colleagues. Such disagreements as on sanctions were very rare. Eden often called at the former chancellor of the exchequer's residence at 11 Downing Street for informal discussions on a variety of issues. But Chamberlain's premiership was to be marked by a growing estrangement, leading to Eden's resignation. By May 1937 Eden had been for years at the centre of foreign policy debate and formulation. Since becoming foreign secretary he had made no progress in his overriding goal of European appeasement. His experiences with the dictators had already mellowed his fervent idealism. His confidence was now tempered by the lessons of broken promises and shattered hopes. The one definite conclusion he had come to was that the key to success in dealing with the dictators lay in firmness and rearmament. He intensified his personal campaign to push forward on the rearmament front by increasing anti-aircraft defences, enlarging the proposed continental army, and expanding the air force.

Chamberlain, in contrast, believed that Britain was wallowing without any definite foreign policy and that the Foreign Office obstructed more direct approaches to Germany and Italy. It was his conviction that war was neither imminent nor inevitable, and that Britain must resist the drift of Europe into contending ideological camps. Unlike Eden, he wished to steer rearmament away from a massive commitment to overwhelming force, towards a programme aimed only at defending Britain and her vital interests against direct attack. He immediately informed Eden that he intended to take more interest than Baldwin had in foreign affairs. Eden reacted with pleasure to the knowledge that he could now share his anxieties at the state of European tension. He was soon to discover, however, how much interest Chamberlain really intended to take in his department.

After failing to improve relations with Germany, Chamberlain turned his attention to Italy, as the weaker partner of the Axis. Relations with Mussolini were particularly strained by the incessant stream of anti-British propaganda, fears of Italy's Mediterranean ambitions, bitterness over the breaches of non-intervention, and Britain's refusal to recognize the Italian conquest of Abyssinia. Eden was willing to help Chamberlain and was not opposed in principle to negotiations. On 19 July he declared in the Commons that there should be no conflict of interest between the two countries in the Mediterranean. However he was privately sceptical, dismissing Mussolini as 'a gangster'. For his part, Mussolini had had his fill of the British foreign secretary and decided to deal directly with Chamberlain. In an exchange of letters at the end of July, Mussolini and Chamberlain assured each other of their wish to normalize Anglo–Italian relations. In a further letter on 27 July, which he did not show Eden, the prime minister made a grave diplomatic error by committing himself to open negotiations with Italy without prior agreement on scope or contents. He had deliberately not shown the letter to Eden, fearing he would object. In fact Eden's disappointment with the 'gentleman's agreement' had convinced him that Italy must first show evidence of good faith before concessions could follow from London.

After a brief vacation in August, Eden returned to the Foreign Office to find a deteriorating situation in the Mediterranean. Plane and submarine attacks against neutral shipping, correctly attributed to the Italians, had increased around the Spanish coast. Spearheaded by careful plans, detailed by Eden and agreed in advance with the French, the Nyon conference opened on 10

September. Both Italy (making the participation of the USSR an excuse) and Germany refused to attend these discussions on the protection of navigation. Eden's skill as an expert negotiator quickly produced agreement by 14 September. The nine participating powers approved a plan to protect shipping routes by naval patrols in designated areas, and made provision for instant counter-attack. Mussolini realized he had made a tactical error in not attending the conference, for it had resulted in an unprecedented display of Anglo–French naval co-operation in the Mediterranean. Italy began patrolling its designated area, and naturally attacks against neutral shipping ceased. Eden was delighted with the success of a conference which had given a much-needed boost to Anglo–French prestige.

Chamberlain acknowledged Eden's success, but was worried that it had been achieved at the expense of Anglo–Italian relations. He had also never abandoned his intention of improving relations with Germany. In November Lord Halifax received an invitation from the German air minister, Field-Marshal Hermann Göring, to attend a hunting exhibition in Berlin. It carried the implication of an opportunity for talks with Hitler, and Chamberlain encouraged acceptance of the invitation. Halifax's return from Germany was eagerly awaited by Eden. He had been sceptical but had not opposed the visit, regarding it only as an informal contact. He had instructed Halifax to avoid any statement which would signify Britain's acquiescence in German demands in either Austria or Czechoslovakia. After analyzing the report on the conversations, Eden came to the conclusion that it had been 'hazardous'. Halifax had hinted at Britain's willingness to recognize Germany's legitimate demands in this area provided they were peacefully pursued. Assessing this episode in *Facing the Dictators*, Eden wrote that the visit should never have been tolerated, for it had weakened his position. The growing differences between him and the prime minister now concerned not strategy but tactics. This rift and rumours of Eden's resignation were becoming a subject of press speculation.

Anglo–French discussions in London on 29 and 30 November did not reveal evidence of these differences. There was general agreement that there would be little popular support for a war against Germany to preserve the independence of Austria and Czechoslovakia. Efforts were therefore to be concentrated on

47

achieving a peaceful settlement. In the case of Czechoslovakia, Eden pointed out, the Sudeten-German minority had certain grievances which deserved fair consideration. He followed these meetings by further conversations in early December with the anglophile Italian ambassador, Count Dino Grandi, and Joachim von Ribbentrop, Hitler's personal choice as German ambassador to London. In neither case could Eden make any progress on outstanding problems. He made it clear to Ribbentrop that particular questions, such as Germany's colonial claims, must be part of a general settlement. With Grandi Eden held to his preconditions that, among other things, anti-British propaganda must cease prior to the recognition of Abyssinia.

A fundamental strategic consideration which the chiefs of staff had impressed on the government was that Britain did not have the resources to be involved simultaneously in Europe and the Far East. This was a pressing problem for Eden because in July Japan had reopened its war of conquest in China. He acknowledged that Britain's inadequate naval resources made action dependent on American co-operation, and he worked incessantly to obtain this in Asia. The nine-power Brussels conference, to which the United States sent a delegate, met from 3 to 24 November. It failed to agree on anything except a resolution condemning Japan's invasion of China. Determined on action, Eden then proposed a joint Anglo–American show of naval forces in the Far East and the opening of staff talks. Both proposals met with disfavour in Washington, where isolationist feeling and neutrality legislation hindered action in foreign spheres. Eden was gratified, however, by the small gesture of co-operation which President Franklin D. Roosevelt approved in allowing the Navy Department to exchange secret information with the Admiralty. Eden remained firmly convinced that on the basis of Anglo–American co-operation world peace could be assured 'without a shot being fired'. Chamberlain, in contrast, was convinced that it was safest to count on nothing from the Americans but words.

On 3 January 1938 Eden and his family left for a vacation in the south of France. In his absence Chamberlain took charge at the Foreign Office. On 11 January the prime minister received details of a startling presidential initiative. Subject to British approval, Roosevelt intended on the 22nd to launch an appeal leading to a world conference to discuss quite general issues such as disarmament, raw materials and the principles of international conduct. It was hoped that this conference would assist Chamberlain's work of European appeasement. Roosevelt's closest advisers had warned him that his initiative, with which they were not happy, might not be welcome in London. In fact it produced bitter controversy and was the beginning of the drama of Eden's resignation. Chamberlain, as he noted in his diary, considered the contents as 'fantastic and likely to excite the derision of Germany and Italy'. On 13 January he asked the president to defer the initiative, arguing that it cut across his own attempts to improve relations with the dictators. Eden had not been consulted on the grounds that transmitting abroad a still secret plan was too risky, and Roosevelt had requested a reply by 17 January.

It was only on 15 January, after having been contacted by telephone, that a hurt and angry Eden returned to London. Roosevelt's gesture, and certainly not its contents, excited his imagination. It appeared to crown his patient efforts to involve the United States, coming as it did after the president's agreement to naval talks. The fact, too, that the prime minister had acted in his absence wounded Eden's professional pride. He immediately sent a mollifying telegram to Washington asking Roosevelt not to consider Chamberlain's reaction as a negative response.

There followed a week of acrimonious debate. A personal confrontation and an exchange of letters between Eden and Chamberlain revealed fundamental differences both with regard to Roosevelt's initiative and the chances for success in negotiations with Italy and Germany. On 18 January Roosevelt agreed to defer his initiative. He added a warning against recognizing Italy's conquest of Abyssinia as Chamberlain had foreshadowed in his original reply. Another discussion between Eden and Chamberlain that day ended in deadlock and even worse: after two hours' wrangling, with both men holding to their positions, Eden suggested that he resign. The entire problem was to be put before the Foreign Policy Committee of the Cabinet. It was during their meeting that Eden first heard of the backstage diplomacy being conducted in Rome. Lady Chamberlain, widow of Sir Austen Chamberlain, the prime minister's half-brother, was a warm admirer from previous days of Mussolini. Her soundings of Italian diplomats had convinced Chamberlain that the moment was ripe for a settlement with Italy and that Eden was an outright impediment.

The issues dividing Chamberlain and Eden were not reflected in the Foreign Policy Committee. Support for the foreign secretary was very limited, but no decision was reached. Foreign Office colleagues were in despair, freely discussing his resignation. They realized that this was impossible without disclosing the still secret Roosevelt plan. Another meeting of the Foreign Policy Committee on 20 January saved the face of both Chamberlain and Eden. Agreement was secured to encourage Roosevelt to go ahead with his initiative at any time he felt was convenient. He was further informed that Britain would proceed with *de jure* recognition of Abyssinia, but only as part of a general settlement with Italy. On 25 January Roosevelt expressed himself satisfied with British policy and later indicated that he had no objections to Anglo–Italian conversations. His initiative, however, was never to be undertaken. This entire episode had especially weakened Eden's position. The issue of his resignation, openly posed and discussed, hung for a week in the balance. It only served to diminish the gesture of protest when it was finally extended.

Chamberlain now felt free to pursue his approaches to both Italy and Germany. A domestic crisis, resulting on 4 February in Hitler assuming the position of supreme military commander and appointing Ribbentrop as foreign minister, impressed even Chamberlain as a portent of extremism. He turned his full attention to Italy. In conversations with Grandi, Eden insisted on the cessation of anti-British propaganda as a prerequisite to the opening of negotiations, and he gave the ambassador details of a scheme for troop withdrawals from Spain. The Cabinet endorsed this approach. Speaking to a meeting at Birmingham on 12 February, Eden declared that a lasting peace depended on making agreements in which there was no sacrifice of principles merely to obtain hasty, but impermanent, results.

Information from Lady Chamberlain and secret contacts between the Italian embassy and 10 Downing Street convinced the prime minister that he should proceed with the conversations. Almost two weeks after he had asked for the meeting, Chamberlain received Grandi on 18 February. Eden, who had prevaricated in fulfilling Chamberlain's request, joined them at 10 Downing Street. The three-hour conversation ranged over a wide field, including the agenda for the projected Anglo–Italian negotiations. Eden's sole intervention elicited from Grandi the admission that the expected Nazi offensive against Austria would not be deterred by hastening the negotiations, and that nothing had been decided about the British formula for troop withdrawals.

Grandi returned later in the day, to be told that a final decision rested with the Cabinet. In the interval, however, Eden had had a vehement row with Chamberlain, who was determined to tell Grandi that talks could begin at once. 'Anthony, you have missed chance after chance. You simply cannot go on like this', the prime minister said. At the Foreign Office Eden told his colleagues that if he could not carry the Cabinet he intended to resign.

Rumours of Cabinet dissensions brought a large crowd into Downing Street on 19 February. Eden had taken no precautions to align Cabinet support or warn backbench opinion. On the other hand Sir John Simon was going around saying that Eden was physically exhausted and mentally ill. Chamberlain knew the strength of his Cabinet support and in any case had already decided to get rid of Eden. The prime minister began by explaining his reasons for wishing to improve relations with Italy and described the meeting with Grandi. Eden followed with a similar account, but stressed his distrust of Mussolini with examples dating back to the 'gentleman's agreement'. He was convinced that Mussolini wanted the negotiations to recover some of his prestige lost because of Austrian developments. Normal diplomatic practice, Eden concluded, required careful advance preparation, cemented by tokens of goodwill. From every point of view it was not the time to open negotiations. As each Cabinet minister was called upon to express his opinion, Eden saw that he had no outright supporters. The Cabinet approved Chamberlain's decision to proceed with the Italian negotiations. Eden replied that he could not support this policy. He wished, therefore, to resign.

For the next twenty-four hours an almost continuous series of discussions, including a session of the Cabinet and a special committee of mediators, failed to find a compromise. At 7.30 p.m. on 20 February Eden notified the Cabinet that his decision was irrevocable. He returned to the Foreign Office to write his letter of resignation. It was accepted by Chamberlain at midnight. Lord Cranbourne, parliamentary under-secretary of state for foreign affairs, and J. P. L. Thomas, Eden's parliamentary private secretary, both personal friends, also resigned.

During a Cabinet meeting that day Chamberlain had passed a

note to Eden suggesting that their differences were not of ultimate principles, but of outlook and methods. This was repeated in their official exchange of letters. It was even mentioned on the afternoon of 21 February, when Eden spoke from the backbenches of a crowded and bewildered House of Commons. He stated that he was not opposed to negotiations with the Italian government. In the light of numerous instances of Italian bad faith, however, he had to look for performance as opposed to promise. He then referred to the differences in outlook and method which separated him from the prime minister. Eden admitted there was no difference on fundamental principles. But, he continued, 'in international affairs can anyone define where outlook and methods end and principles begin?' He had recently become convinced that Britain was over-anxious to make terms with others rather than to be offered terms. He concluded: 'I do not believe that we can make progress in European appeasement . . . if we allow the impression to gain currency abroad that we yield to constant pressure.'

Although the speech was punctuated by cheers, mainly from opposition MPs, it was not one of Eden's better parliamentary performances. He was restrained and noticeably tense, with a self-conscious posture about pleading that differences not of principle but of method had forced him to resign. Even if, as he had politely suggested, the grounds between the two were blurred, method in foreign policy belongs to the competence of the foreign secretary. And Chamberlain had insisted on intruding in that area. That in itself does not strengthen Eden's decision. He had previously confronted issues for resignation and had compromised. But a basic flaw in his character, which was to emerge again at the time of the Suez crisis in 1956, made him a prisoner of his own strong and principled convictions. He could not as yet have realized that his resignation saved his reputation. From his first test as foreign minister at the time of the Rhineland crisis, he had been committed to a policy of appeasement. It was only after his departure from office that Chamberlain's appeasement policies earned a derogatory connotation. Eden's resignation left his reputation intact both at home and abroad, and untainted by the events which led to World War II.

Eden had now broken with the government and alienated much of the Conservative party establishment. However he still had an enormous personal following. Many hoped he would provide a strong focus for discontent with the national government's policies. Unfortunately they were to be disappointed. In a speech to his constituents at Leamington on 25 February he stated that the government must pursue its chosen policies, 'and neither by word nor deed do I desire now to say anything to make their task more difficult'. Chamberlain and Lord Halifax, who succeeded Eden at the Foreign Office, privately congratulated him on the restraint he had shown.

Eden was to fulfil his Leamington pledge completely. It was not within his character to repudiate the Conservative establishment which had advanced his career, notwithstanding his undoubted talents. In addition, to have joined the critics of the government would have implied repudiation of his own work as foreign secretary, undertaken to further European appeasement. With patience and restraint, and given the parlous state of European relations, he must have known that he would eventually return to the government.

On 13 March, when German troops occupied Vienna, Hitler succeeded in his long-cherished ambition of uniting Germany and Austria. This was followed by the conclusion on 16 April of the Anglo–Italian agreement. In exchange for British *de jure* recognition of the conquest of Abyssinia, Mussolini undertook to withdraw his troops from Spain after the civil war. Only then would the agreement come into force. Eden regarded the agreement as a repetition of promises previously made and repeatedly broken.

Eden did not comment publicly on either of these major international events. As a result of soundings in various quarters, he decided to watch events from the sidelines and make no political speeches. He frequently consulted Baldwin, who had in fact advised him to adopt this low profile approach. It was Baldwin, too, who freely spoke of Eden as the next prime minister. Eden followed his suggestions to immerse himself in domestic affairs. He studied the unemployment problems in his constituency, visited armament factories and economically depressed areas, and began writing for the American press. He did not however cut himself off from politics. His relations with Halifax remained intimate. Eden could count on being kept accurately informed on trends in government policy both from Halifax and Oliver Harvey, his adoring former private secretary at the Foreign Office.

It was only in May that Eden began to attend regularly at the

House of Commons, and it was another two months before he made his first political speech since his resignation. His stand had if anything increased his popularity in the House, where the growing lack of confidence in Chamberlain created pockets of MPs critical of the government. Some gravitated naturally to the charismatic leadership of Winston Churchill and joined in his critical barrages. Although he had not always agreed with Eden, by 1935 Churchill had regarded him as 'the only good member of the government'. They formed a mutual regard, and their views on foreign policy increasingly coincided. Churchill later confessed that Eden's resignation caused his only sleepless night in a lifetime of crises. It was Baldwin's advice, however, that convinced Eden to steer clear of Churchill, thus avoiding the role of second fiddle. This decision was confirmed by intimations from Chamberlain and Halifax that his eventual return to the Cabinet would be welcomed. For the time being Eden politely declined.

Czechoslovakia now followed Spain as Europe's crisis area. Eden had hoped, as did Chamberlain, that Berlin and Prague could amicably settle the demands for autonomy of the Sudeten-German minority within Czechoslovakia. By early September this hope seemed unrealizable. Eden twice consulted with Halifax, urging him to inform Hitler that if the dispute with Czechoslovakia led to war, and if France was involved as a result of her treaty of mutual assistance with Czechoslovakia, then Britain could not avoid involvement. Chamberlain's approach still consisted of finding a negotiated settlement. In pursuit of this he twice visited Germany to meet Hitler at Berchtesgaden and then at Godesberg. The demands Hitler made at Godesberg on 24 September gave rise to a serious Cabinet dispute and public debate as to the limits to which Czechoslovakia could be pressed. Eden was appalled at the severity of the terms, capable of virtually destroying the Czech state. While he was not opposed to appeasement, he had told his constituents at Stratford-upon-Avon on 23 September, it must not be at the expense of Britain's vital interests, reputation, or sense of fair dealing. Even Halifax was now brought to the brink of opposition to Chamberlain.

On 28 September the prime minister dramatically announced in the House that he was to meet Hitler, Mussolini, and the French prime minister, Edouard Daladier, at Munich. While MPs rose to cheer, Eden left the chamber. The following day Churchill prepared to warn Chamberlain not to extract further concessions from the Czechs at the risk of open revolt in the Commons. The signatories of this telegram, besides Churchill, were to have been Clem Attlee, leader of the Labour party, Archibald Sinclair, the Liberal leader, and Eden. Attlee and Sinclair refused to sign. So, too, did Eden on the grounds that it would be interpreted as a vendetta against Chamberlain. Eden had already let it be known, to the disappointment of his many admirers, that he had no intention to lead an anti-government revolt or agitate for resignations from the Cabinet.

Chamberlain returned to London on 30 September to universal acclaim at having achieved a settlement and avoided war. In the parliamentary debate which followed, criticism obtruded into the praise. Duff Cooper explained his reasons for resigning from the Cabinet. Eden reserved his attack for the new Munich terms. On the basis of 'stand and deliver', he declared, war had been avoided at the expense of Czechoslovakia. 'Successive surrenders bring only successive humiliation, and they, in turn, more humiliating demands.' In a candid passage in *Facing the Dictators*, Eden admitted that he had never blamed the British and French governments for not supporting Czechoslovakia to the point of war. In the vote on the government's handling of the crisis, he abstained along with twenty-one other MPs.

In the aftermath of the Munich conference, Chamberlain refused suggestions to broaden the basis of his government by including Churchill and Eden. Talks continued for some time, however, for new elections to produce a more representative national government to unite the nation, hasten rearmament, and speed social reforms. Eden decided that he would stand as an independent Conservative. A series of speeches he delivered in various parts of the country included a welcome analysis of domestic problems besides the usual critique of foreign policy. He flatly rejected suggestions that he either form a new party or lead a breakaway movement from the Conservative party. In all this post-Munich ferment he did nothing to alienate himself from the government. But he soon assumed the leadership of a mainly young group of MPs known as 'the Eden group'. The government whips' office scathingly described them as 'the glamour boys'. They met at irregular intervals until the outbreak of war and acted not as a conspiratorial minority but as a ginger group trying to influence government policy. Membership numbered about thirty, including Harold Macmillan, Leo Amery, J. P. L. Thomas, Lord Cranbourne, Harold Nicolson, Richard Law, Ronald Tree, and Duff Cooper.

On 2 November the Anglo-Italian agreement was ratified by the House of Commons. Eden challenged this decision on the grounds that the preconditions for its implementation had not been fulfilled. Italian intervention in Spain had in fact intensified. Chamberlain regarded the agreement as helping to improve the cordial relations he had established at Munich with Mussolini. On the other hand, Anglo–German relations deteriorated when, as a result of a murder at the German embassy in Paris, a violent pogrom was unleashed against German Jews. Hitler now added Eden to his list of British warmongers, lumping him with Churchill and Duff Cooper as associates of 'the international of Jews and Freemasons'.

After much delay Eden accepted in late November an invitation to address the Annual Congress of American Industry in New York. He let it be known before leaving that he would not criticize his government in the United States, where his resignation had been closely followed. He and his wife arrived in New York to a welcome befitting a film star rather than a politician. Everywhere he was followed by the curious and interested, to whom he appeared the epitome of the Englishman – only the umbrella was missing. On 9 December he made his scheduled speech, a quick survey of international affairs since the war and some comments on democracy. This was followed by conversations in Washington with State Department officials and a meeting with Roosevelt. The events of the previous January were not mentioned. Afterwards Eden reflected that while Roosevelt had displayed all the charm he had been led to expect, he knew the president no better than before. The week's visit was a personal success for Eden which, true to his word, gave the British government no cause for anxiety.

1939 began with Chamberlain and Halifax visiting Rome, followed on their return with a major war scare over reports of an intended German attack westwards. It was on 15 March, however, that the German army proceeded to occupy the remnants of the post-Munich Czech state. The suddenness of Hitler's betrayal of his Munich assurances of peaceful intentions had historic repercussions. Within a month Chamberlain had revolutionized British foreign policy. On 31 March he guaranteed the independence of Poland, followed by similar guarantees on 13 April to Romania and Greece. For the first time since World War 1 Britain had treaty obligations in eastern Europe.

Some of the credit for this firm British stand was due to the dissident parliamentary voices of the Churchill and Eden groups. On 16 March Eden had spoken in the Commons of the need for an all-party government of national unity. He exhorted the government to co-operate with the peaceful states of Europe against further German aggression. According to Harold Nicolson, who was recording in his diaries the meetings of the group, for a brief moment Eden seemed poised to revolt openly against the government. On 27 March the Eden and Churchill groups combined to table a motion asking for the introduction of conscription, the formation of a broad coalition government, and the reorganization of industry on a wartime basis. The guarantee to Poland and the decision to double the Territorial Army convinced the groups to withdraw their motion.

The transformed map of European diplomatic alignments tempted Eden to re-enter the government. Halifax, as always, was amenable and openly canvassed on his behalf. Chamberlain again refused, regarding Eden's or, indeed, Churchill's return to the Cabinet as symbolizing an irrevocable belief in the inevitability of war. Chamberlain still hoped that the deterrent front Britain was forging in eastern Europe might succeed. Negotiations had opened in mid-April for an agreement on mutual assistance between Britain, France and the Soviet Union. For more than a month little progress was evident. On 19 May, in a Commons debate on foreign affairs, Eden joined in the powerful chorus of speeches from Churchill and Lloyd George urging the government to conclude its negotiations with the USSR and thereby add military strength to the guarantees. Eden then took a more positive initiative. As the only British minister to have visited Moscow, he told Halifax on 3 June that perhaps his influence with Stalin might hasten the negotiations. The foreign secretary liked the idea of sending Eden to Moscow. Fortunately the proposal was vetoed by Chamberlain. It was a risky suggestion with little hope of success.

At the end of June another 'week-end crisis' threatened the continent. It appeared that Hitler was about to realize his next aim of reincorporating within the Reich the free city of Danzig on the

Baltic. 'The Eden group' had received supporting intelligence that Hitler was poised to act. They decided that a reconstruction of the Cabinet, bringing in Eden and Churchill, would deter Hitler, and enlisted the help of *The Daily Telegraph* to launch such a campaign. It failed to impress Chamberlain. In any case, Hitler had not yet been ready to take Danzig.

Parliament was scheduled to adjourn on 4 August for its summer recess. The international situation was still unsettled. A Nazi coup in Danzig was expected at any moment, and negotiations continued with the Soviet Union. Harold Nicolson had for some time been dissatisfied with Eden's cautious approach to contentious issues. The group feared above all that Chamberlain would again weaken and the Danzig dispute would result in another Munich, this time at Polish expense. 'If only Anthony Eden would now come out in rage against this subversive attempt', Nicolson wrote in his diary on 18 July. 'But Anthony does not wish to defy the Tory Party and is in fact missing every boat with exquisite elegance.' The group had originally decided to vote against the government in the adjournment debate. At the last moment Eden and most of his dissident colleagues toed the line.

Eden realized that in the event of war, and with no firm prospect of office, he could not rule out active military service. On 29 April he had been commissioned in the Territorial Army as a major in the 2nd battalion, the Rangers, King's Royal Rifle Corps, his old regiment. The battalion was earmarked for work as an armoured unit, part of the 1st, and at that time the only, Armoured Division. After parliament adjourned, therefore, Eden lived under canvas and exercised during August with his battalion on Salisbury Plain. It was here that on the morning of the 24th he read the newspaper reports that the Soviet Union had abandoned its negotiations with Britain and France and concluded a non-aggression pact with Germany.

War now seemed inevitable. Eden returned immediately to London and spoke later that day to an emergency sitting of the House of Commons. He indulged in no recriminations, only pointing out that concessions to Germany had never been reciprocated. He expressed precisely the mood of the House when in conclusion he stated that, having given a pledge to Poland, there could be no turning back. On 30 August, in a broadcast to the United States, he declared that 'we cannot live for ever at the pistol point.' For civilization depended on the maintenance of certain standards of international conduct.

On 1 September, as Germany launched its attack against Poland, Eden visited his battalion, which was protecting bridges over the Thames. Throughout that day and the next he contemplated his future. Churchill had already been offered a Cabinet post. In the early hours of 2 September he wrote to Chamberlain saying that Eden's entry into the Cabinet was vital as he represented moderate Conservative opinion. By 3 September there was still no news from Chamberlain. 'The Eden group' met at 11 a.m. to hear the prime minister announce that Britain was at war with Germany. Eden's summons to 10 Downing Street eventually came in the afternoon. Chamberlain explained that he wanted a small War Cabinet. Therefore he could only offer Eden the position of secretary of state for the dominions, without a Cabinet seat but with access on relevant occasions. Under the impact of war, Eden felt compelled to accept.

3

'LIKE A MAN GOING HOME'

1939-1945

ANTHONY EDEN went to work for the first time at the Dominions Office on 4 September 1939. It was not the position he would have wished. Nor did the office, with its limited access to the Cabinet, fulfil his expectations for his eventual return to the government. In *The Reckoning* he candidly described his position in the Cabinet as 'anomalous and humiliating'. But for the following eight months he dutifully co-ordinated the commonwealth contribution to the war. Australia, New Zealand, the Union of South Africa and Canada shortly announced their decision to stand by Britain in the fight against Nazi Germany. Eire opted for a policy of neutrality.

The high commissioners in London were delighted that such a prominent politician was looking after their affairs. Eden established an easy rapport with them and relations were rarely strained. From the beginning they decided on a format of consultation which symbolized the role the commonwealth was to fulfil throughout the war. It was agreed that he would meet them every day, including Sundays if necessary, to consult and exchange information. These meetings became known as the 'junior War Cabinet'.

Prior to the outbreak of war the high commissioners had fought tenaciously, within the limits of their influence, for an Anglo–German settlement at almost any cost. When Hitler completed his subjugation of Poland, peace proposals were expected from Berlin. Eden took the high commissioners into the government's confidence and reported their desires for Britain to be more forthcoming in its reply to Hitler. The high commissioners were largely unsuccessful and the British reply to Hitler remained firm and uncompromising. It contained no definite statement of war aims. Eden personally gave a lot of thought both at this time and throughout the war to this thorny question. Later in the year he defined these as having two aspects. On the negative side he looked forward to the total destruction of Hitlerism and Nazi rule in Europe. On the positive side he hoped that after the war Europe would be organized along the lines of some sort of federation, comprising a defence scheme, a customs union and common currency.

The early months of Commonwealth co-operation with Britain witnessed, under Eden's management, a very impressive contribution. He endorsed a plan which emanated from the Canadian high commissioner, Vincent Massey, and the Australian high commissioner, Stanley Bruce. The Massey–Bruce scheme envisaged British, Australian and New Zealand air crews being trained in Canada and then sent to the front for active service. Eden pressed the scheme on Neville Chamberlain and the Commonwealth Air Training Programme was thus born. Pilots and navigators in their thousands were trained and made a substantial contribution to final victory.

At the end of October Eden acted as host to a meeting of dominion representatives in London. The highlight of the gathering was a tour of inspection of the front lines in France and a meeting with the French prime minister, Edouard Daladier. Although Eden was impressed by the morale of the two British divisions on the front, as he reported to the Cabinet on his return, he voiced concern at their lack of equipment and the extended front for which they were responsible. At least one commonwealth minister came back to report that the Germans would go through the Anglo–French lines like a knife through cheese.

During a small government reconstruction in January 1940 Churchill strongly pressed the case for Eden to be put in charge of the War Office. Eden would have loved this ministry as it would put him closer to the centre of military events. He also felt he was being insufficiently occupied in the Dominions Office, and would have preferred an executive department. But Chamberlain was against it, and so Eden continued with his Dominions Office duties. He travelled to Greenock in Scotland to welcome the arrival of the first Canadian division to come to Europe. In early February he visited Cairo to meet Australian and New Zealand troops arriving there. A meeting with King Farouk confirmed some of the disturbing information Eden had gathered from other sources. Despite his assurances that Mussolini intended to abide by his declaration of neutrality, King Farouk remained suspicious of Italy and worried about her massive strengthening of the defences of Libya.

On 9 April Germany invaded Norway, marking the end of the period known as the 'phoney war'. The abysmal performance of British forces trying to counter this successful German operation led to the downfall of the Chamberlain government with important consequences for Eden. A two-day parliamentary debate on the situation developed into an enquiry on Chamberlain's suitability to conduct the war. In the vote at the end of the debate on 8 May the prime minister's majority fell. Ninety-three Conservatives either voted against the government or abstained. Churchill calmly waited for the summons from the king. On 9 May he dined with Eden, promising him the War Office. The next day, which began with news of the German invasion of Holland and Belgium, Chamberlain finally resigned. Winston Churchill was summoned to Buckingham Palace and asked to form a new government. On 12 May Eden, appointed secretary of state for war, was sworn in along with other Cabinet ministers at the palace. Owing to new regulations they had to take the oath of office, not from the king, but, ironically, from Chamberlain, the new lord president of the council.

That same day Eden had his final meeting with the dominion high commissioners who deeply regretted his departure. Fortunately, the broad lines of commonwealth co-operation had already been established. In the afternoon Eden moved to the War Office where he had his first meeting with the chief of the imperial general staff, General Sir Edmund Ironside. He noted later in his diary the impression that Eden was taking over at a difficult time, though he seemed strong enough in character.

The momentum of Germany's first thrust westwards held few laurels for a British minister in charge of a retreating army. Moreover, Churchill was also minister for defence. As such he controlled the overall direction of the war, for his office had undefined scope and limitless power. This inevitably led to the subordination of the three service ministers to Churchill's dictates. Nevertheless, Eden was pleased that he was now closer to the centre of power and his brief career as war minister was to have its dramatic highlights.

With Germany advancing through Holland, Belgium and France, the threat of imminent invasion became acute. The successful use of German paratroops in Holland drew the sombre lesson that the civilian population had to be prepared to resist this new force. Eden's first task at the War Office was to broadcast plans, previously prepared and approved by the Cabinet on 12 May, for what he then called 'The Local Defence Volunteers'. It was Churchill who persuaded him to adopt the more imaginative and emotive name of 'Home Guard'. The response was overwhelming. Fortunately, the test of this force, described by Eden to the Cabinet as the 'broomstick army', never arrived.

Eden shared the general gloom in London that Britain's last ally on the continent was on the verge of defeat. Germany's armour and dive-bombers sliced through France, towards the sea and on to Paris. The British Expeditionary Force (BEF) withdrew to the Channel ports. On 26 May Eden agreed to one of the most heartbreaking decisions of the war. He ordered, on Churchill's command, that the surrounded British troops in Calais should continue to resist and would not be evacuated. This move was to delay the German armoured advance along the coast to Dunkirk. Among the troops left to surrender or die at Calais was a battalion of Eden's World War I regiment, the King's Royal Rifle Corps. By the end of May Eden was preparing plans for the withdrawal of the entire BEF from France. On 2 June he broadcast to the nation: he reported the safe evacuation of the bulk of the BEF from Dunkirk, and described in vivid detail the 'Battle of the Ports'. Almost immediately he threw himself into the immense task of re-equipping a battered army which had returned to England shorn of virtually all its equipment.

On 11 June Eden accompanied Churchill to a meeting of the Anglo–French Supreme War Council. The battle for France was reaching its climax. At the meeting at Briare, near Orléans, Eden heard Churchill declare that Britain would continue the fight even after France fell. On 14 June German troops entered Paris.

The fall of France heightened the threat of an invasion of Britain. At the same time, Italy had entered the war as an ally of Germany. This increased the danger which Italian forces posed to Britain's position in Egypt and the Sudan. As a result of this, a tenacious battle of wits developed during the summer between

Churchill and Eden. The prime minister was mainly concerned with the defence of Britain, for which he was prepared to denude the Middle East of troops and equipment. Eden was more worried about the Italian threat from Libya and Abyssinia. He was convinced that only in North Africa could Britain come to grips with the enemy and emerge triumphant. In the end he was proved right. Eden was strongly supported throughout by General Sir A. P. Wavell, commander-in-chief of the Middle East, a soldier disliked by the prime minister, but whose abilities and quiet manner Eden found attractive. Eden reciprocated Wavell's support and regard, even to the point of threatening Churchill with his own resignation should Wavell continue to be singled out for criticism.

Although Churchill could be heavy-handed and exigent in dealing with Eden, he was also considerate of his problems. In early July Churchill had agreed to establish a small Cabinet committee to handle Middle Eastern problems. The committee, presided over by Eden, recommended on 28 July the dispatch of another armoured division to the Middle East and further reinforcements of Australian and New Zealand troops. Eden then brought Wavell to London in early August for consultations. The prime minister still doubted Wavell's vigour and resolve, but the talks succeeded in approving the dispatch of further forces to the Middle East. In *The Second World War* Churchill gave no indication of the dispute leading to this decision, while in *The Reckoning* Eden gave himself and the War Office credit for this decisive act, though paying tribute to Churchill, for his was the final responsibility.

The Battle of Britain began on 13 August. In June Eden had rented a house on the downs near Dover. From this observation post he paid regular visits to local commanders and on weekends had a front seat view of the air battles overhead. The expected land invasion however did not materialize. By the end of September Eden again began to agitate for further convoys of armour and aircraft to the Middle East. In late August vehement arguments had developed between him and the prime minister on this subject. Eden found his attitude 'really maddening'. He told Churchill that he was forever nagging at the army. Churchill had already told Eden that he was succumbing to a 'weary departmentalism', and in any case he was far harder on the navy. But relations between the two men, founded on a basis of mutual trust and confidence, never soured. By forceful argument tempered with respectful deference Eden often got his way. Churchill and the Defence Committee agreed at the end of September to Eden's latest request for Middle East reinforcements.

On 6 October the War Cabinet heard the news of Churchill's sudden decision to send Eden on a mission to the Middle East. He was to assess the exact position in Egypt and North Africa. Churchill was worried about what he called the 'general slackness' of the Middle East command in concentrating troops for battle. He knew he could count on Eden to put forward his views on the spot.

Delighted with the scope of his mission, Eden arrived in Cairo on 14 October. He launched into an intensive round of consultations with Wavell and Lieutenant-General Sir Henry Wilson who had been a First World War staff officer in the 41st division which included Eden's battalion. Dispositions in the western desert, Italy's probable intentions, present counteraction and future plans were outlined and discussed. Eden telegraphed to Churchill on the imperative need for further reinforcements of planes and tanks. Churchill sent a reassuring reply. He urged Eden not to hasten his return but continue to master the local situation. Eden then toured Palestine and Transjordan, inspecting British troops and the desert patrol of colourfully dressed Bedouin Arabs.

On the morning of 28 October Italian troops and aircraft from occupied Albania attacked Greece, a country guaranteed by Britain in April 1939. That morning, too, Eden had scheduled a flight to take him to a meeting with the South African prime minister, General Jan Christian Smuts, in Khartoum. Eden spent four days in discussions there. Meanwhile, Churchill had decided at all costs to prevent Crete from falling into Italian hands. He was prepared to run any risk and wanted reinforcements from the Middle East sent there. Eden, who by 1 November had returned to Cairo, held other views. Firstly, he believed that the defence of Egypt was the crux of Britain's military position in the Middle East, and that resources from this area would not influence the war in Greece. Secondly, ever since his meeting with Wavell and Wilson in Cairo, Eden had been informed of plans for a British offensive in the western desert. This was revealed to Eden in such secrecy that he had to bear in silence the brunt of a tirade of telegrams from Churchill without being able to reply.

It was imperative for Eden to return immediately to London.

He hinted at the important news in a telegram to Churchill on 1 November and at last succeeded in convincing the prime minister to allow him to return. He reached London on 8 November and met Churchill, then working in a disused underground station near Piccadilly. There he unfolded in detail the carefully guarded plans of Wavell and Wilson. It was the operation to be codenamed 'Compass': a daring offensive against Marshal Rodolfo Graziani's army of 80,000 troops, strung out in a series of fortified desert camps. Churchill was delighted with this news. 'I purred like six cats,' he wrote in *The Second World War*. A telegram was sent the next day to Wavell assuring him of all necessary support.

Eden's Middle East mission had been a triumphant success. He had made only one mistake, forgetting to enquire the date for 'Compass'. Churchill was impatient and again became critical of Wavell. At last on the morning of 9 December Wilson launched his attack and in a series of dazzling advances reached Benghazi, crushing the Italian army which had stood poised to conquer Egypt. But by then Eden was no longer in command of the War Office.

On several occasions since the summer Churchill had discussed possible Cabinet changes with Eden, who always replied that he preferred to stay at the War Office rather than become foreign secretary again with a seat in the War Cabinet. On 30 September Churchill revealed further that he would not carry on after the war and, as Eden recorded in his diary, 'the succession would be mine'.

In early December the highly successful British ambassador to Washington, Lord Lothian, died. With a suitable vacancy thus created for Lord Halifax, Churchill insisted that Eden return to the Foreign Office, with additional duties on the Defence Committee. Eden had no choice but to accept. He looked back in *The Reckoning* on his seven months at the War Office as a period when 'every day and often every hour had been crammed with historic incident. My heart had been in the work.' There is no doubt that he was reluctant to leave the War Office. But as Churchill wrote in *The Second World War*, Eden returned to the Foreign Office 'like a man going home'. There seems equally no doubt that Churchill, who took an absorbing interest in military matters, was finding Eden's independence at the War Office a cause of too-frequent differences. It is true, as Churchill wrote, that Eden's tenure of the War Office had brought them closer together. They did think alike on many issues, and during the remainder of the war enjoyed an agreeable comradeship. Nine times out of ten, as both were to boast in later years, they did agree. But as Oliver Lyttelton, later Lord Chandos and a Cabinet colleague for many years, observed in his memoirs, Eden's manner and appearance concealed the inflexible nature of his principles on high matters of state. Lyttelton never saw Eden abandon for expediency a principle in which he believed. Consequently, despite Churchill and Eden's father–son relationship, by 1945 Eden was seriously doubting whether he would continue at the Foreign Office. The work still intrigued him. He just could not stand what he described as 'the racket with Winston at all hours'.

These were still the early stages of a war in which Britain was only just holding its own militarily. Diplomacy was directly dependant on military results. When Eden returned to the Foreign Office on 23 December his prospects for influencing events were greatly circumscribed. They were further limited by Churchill's domination not of the formulation, but the implementation of policy. Finally, the fact that the government was a coalition enhanced the influence of the War Cabinet and its various committees.

January 1941 provided a brief period of satisfaction to Britain. Wavell continued his advance against the Italian army on the North African coast. The Greeks, after repelling the first Italian attacks, had counter-attacked across the Albanian border. Hitler, however, was preparing plans to send Mussolini reinforcements for the war in North Africa. While in the Balkans a build-up of German forces in Bulgaria threatened Greece, Yugoslavia and Turkey. Eden was convinced that the key to the whole situation was Turkey. He made this clear both in the War Cabinet, the Defence Committee and privately to Churchill. If a choice had to be made between assisting either Greece, guaranteed by Britain in April 1939, or Turkey, he preferred Turkey. For that country was the buttress of Britain's defences in the eastern Mediterranean.

The Defence Committee on 10 February decided to defend Greece with a generous offer of men and material. Eden and the new chief of the imperial general staff, Lieutenant-General Sir John Dill, were sent to Cairo to co-ordinate the work involved in this fateful decision. Eden was empowered to act on his own in case of emergency; authority for his actions was only afterwards to be approved by the Cabinet. Wavell was ordered to halt his advance at Benghazi, captured on 8 February, and turn his attention to strengthening resistance in the Balkans against the expected German advance.

Bad weather delayed Eden's arrival in Cairo until 19 February. After an intensive round of consultations with the commanders there, Eden telegraphed to Churchill, describing the help that could be given to the Greeks from the resources in the Middle East. On the principle of defending the Greeks he had obviously changed his mind. He threw himself whole-heartedly into the attempt to make at least a show of defending Greece in the hope that it would stiffen the resistance of Yugoslavia and Turkey. On 22 February he and Dill flew to Athens. There they found that the Greek king and government welcomed British help and agreed with the military plans. These were fully approved on 24 February by the War Cabinet in London.

The next stop on Eden's tour was the Turkish capital, Ankara. The government there pointed out that they were inadequately armed and preferred to remain out of the war. During all this time Eden had tried unsuccessfully to make personal contact with the Yugoslav government to concert defensive plans. These advances were rejected. The Yugoslavs did not wish to provoke Hitler.

Eden returned to Athens on 2 March to find that Bulgaria had allied itself with Germany, whose military forces were openly moving into the country. More distressing was the failure of the Greeks, not entirely through their own fault, to deploy along the lines agreed with Eden and Dill. But the die was cast. A united Balkan front had eluded Eden's best efforts, the Germans were poised to attack, and the British government remained committed to making a brave show of defending the lost Greek cause. On 7 March Eden, disguising his anxiety, wrote to Churchill: 'to have fought and suffered in Greece would be less damaging to us than to have left Greece to her fate.' The Cabinet had agreed and accepted full responsibility that same day. On 25 March Eden began his homeward journey. In Malta two days later he heard of the coup d'état in Belgrade against the government's pro-Hitler policies. He returned immediately to Cairo. Hitler reacted violently to the coup. On 6 April he began the air bombardment of Belgrade which flattened the city, and simultaneously the German army invaded both Yugoslavia and Greece.

Behind the decision to help Greece lay the assumption that the forces remaining in the western desert could hold off a possible attack. During the first days of April it had become a calamitous miscalculation. General Erwin Rommel launched his Afrika Korps on a daring counter-attack against the previously won British gains. Eden was downhearted when he reached London on 10 April. He had been gone for almost two months, on a mission which had proved both complex and dramatic. Enormous consequences flowed from the decisions taken at that time. Rommel drove the British army almost back into Egypt. Yugoslavia surrendered on 17 April, followed a week later by Greece. Over 50,000 troops had to be evacuated. These events aroused a storm of criticism. On 6 May Eden defended the decision to help Greece in the House of Commons.

'In this war we are fighting not for gains, but for causes; and Greece is the embodiment of those causes', he stated. General Wolfe's dictum, he continued, that 'war is an option of difficulties' would remain true until British strength was sufficient to make the odds even. He admitted privately, however, that he would be reluctant to go again on a similar mission. He told Churchill: 'I had already lost enough feathers.'

In the following weeks Eden succumbed to the doldrums into which events had cast diplomacy. In early June, however, he was instrumental in encouraging the tricky operation of allowing a combined British and Free French force to invade Syria, nominally under the rule of the Vichy French Government, but threatened by a possible German takeover. This successful operation protected the Turks on their southern frontier, secured the route to Iraq, and defended the eastern flank of the British armies in Egypt. Meanwhile, Eden began work on a far-reaching reform of the Foreign Office and Diplomatic and Consular Service. The three branches were to be combined, increasing efficiency, abolishing the former exclusiveness of the Service, and establishing its complete independence from all other government departments.

During this time too, Eden bought the lease of Binderton, near Chichester, a seventeenth-century brick and stone cottage. It was the first country home the Edens had ever owned, and it remained in their possession until 1952. It proved an ideal retreat for a man like Eden with a tendency to overwork. Here he snatched an occasional weekend away from the Foreign Office, the House of Commons and the urgent summons from Churchill. He was able to entertain such old friends as Lord Cranbourne and J. P. L. Thomas, and engage in intimate conversation such new acquaintances as the American ambassador, John G. Winant. Here, too, Eden indulged his love of gardening and the countryside.

These few weeks of relative ease were suddenly swept away in the dawn hours of 22 June. Earlier in the month Eden had warned the scheming but likeable Soviet ambassador in London, Ivan Maisky, of intelligence indicating a German attack against the Soviet Union. These warnings were ignored. Eden was staying with Churchill at Chequers when he was awoken with the news of the German attack against the USSR. Churchill immediately assured the Russians of British support. Eden returned to London to discuss with Maisky a whole range of questions regarding military and economic assistance. The alliance that had failed to be concluded in 1939 was soon to be achieved, but in conditions of greater difficulty and under the strain of world war.

Anglo–Soviet relations provided Eden with some of his most testing experiences as wartime foreign secretary. He had always been on good terms with Maisky and prided himself on the success of his 1935 visit to Stalin. The war years were to confirm his original impression of Stalin as a mild-mannered dictator but a ruthless negotiator. Eden's assurances, following the German attack, that Britain was as determined as ever to fight for the defeat of Nazi Germany led on 12 July to the signature of an Anglo–Soviet agreement on mutual assistance. It provided for military and economic support and bound both countries not to conclude a separate peace. Questions of political co-operation, first raised by the Kremlin, were momentarily excluded. As a consequence of this agreement, Eden's patient diplomacy and good offices enabled the Poles and Russians to agree on military co-operation and the annulment of previous German–Soviet treaties affecting Poland.

During July and August close watch was kept on the steadily advancing German blitzkrieg on Russia. Few people, including Eden, held out much hope of a prolonged resistance. As the fighting intensified, Russia proved to be a voracious ally. Stalin bombarded London with requests for material aid, for British troops to fight in the Caucasus, and for the opening of a second front in western Europe. Both Eden and Churchill spent hours with Maisky during September explaining that Britain was suffering from limited military resources but unlimited demands. Nor was the shipping available to land a large enough army in France, with adequate air cover, to draw any appreciable German forces away from the Eastern Front. Nevertheless, supplies of armaments and strategic raw materials were stepped up.

The military situation in Russia continued to deteriorate. Half of the Soviet Ukraine was occupied, and the German armies pressed on to the lower Don. In the north Leningrad was encircled and Moscow was already under attack. Stalin's demands for assistance escalated. The exchanges between Moscow and London became harsh. Stalin demanded a clear answer on unresolved questions affecting war aims, the post-war settlement and close military collaboration. This impasse in Anglo–Soviet relations appealed to Eden's vanity. On 4 November he suggested to Churchill the idea of a visit to Moscow. The prime minister, who was then taking a tough line with Stalin, preferred to wait until the Russians would roll out the red carpet for his foreign secretary. Possibly remembering his last Middle East mission, Eden also hesitated, wishing to see the political ground thoroughly prepared beforehand. At last on 21 November Churchill relented and Eden appeared satisfied. The Cabinet agreed on condition that the foreign secretary was to avoid discussions on post-war frontiers. Stalin was warned in advance of this restriction on the talks.

Eden prepared to leave on 7 December for his Arctic journey to the Soviet Union. He was accompanied by a strong Foreign Office team, in addition to staff officers from the War Office and the Air Ministry. Just as he was sailing, he received the news, direct from Churchill, that Japan had attacked the US Pacific fleet at Pearl Harbour. Eden could not conceal his relief. He felt that it was now only a question of time. Later he observed in *The Reckoning*: 'Before we had believed in the end but never seen the means, now both were clear.' Churchill immediately set off to confer with Roosevelt. Eden continued his journey to Moscow, where he arrived on 15 December.

The foreign secretary had in fact gone to Moscow with very little room for manoeuvre. Roosevelt had insisted that Britain was not to enter into any secret agreement with the Soviet Union in regard to post-war territorial arrangements in Europe. Eden hoped therefore to pin down Stalin to a general declaration of intent, along the lines of the Atlantic Charter signed by Roosevelt and Churchill in August. Stalin unfortunately wanted a firm agreement. He spelled

71

out his plans for frontier changes in Europe which would give the Soviet Union cast-iron guarantees for her security. As Stalin put it at their first meeting, he regarded a declaration as mere algebra, but an agreement was 'practical arithmetic'. Throughout the war Stalin never wavered in his preference for 'practical arithmetic'.

Despite Eden's most conciliatory negotiating techniques, Stalin remained unmoved. He now insisted openly on the immediate recognition of Soviet Russia's 1941 frontiers. In effect this meant recognition of Soviet occupation of parts of Finland, the Baltic States, Bessarabia, and a substantial portion of eastern Poland. Eden was unable to convince him that such a far-reaching agreement needed further consultations with the Cabinet, the dominions and the United States.

The conversations were temporarily broken off. Eden and his party were taken to inspect the front lines and visited Tchaikovsky's house. The day's rest from the negotiations proved beneficial, for when Eden attended the final talks on 20 December, Stalin conceded that he understood Britain's need for extensive consultations. He dropped his demand for immediate recognition of Russia's 1941 frontiers. The visit ended with a sumptuous evening banquet, followed by a film show. In the early hours of the morning Eden telegraphed to Churchill with a note of well-deserved satisfaction. The mission, with limited aims, had produced useful results. The consultations had ended on a friendly note, Eden wrote. Soviet suspicions had been partially allayed. Stalin's demands for immediate frontier recognition had been resisted, at least for the time. The position of Britain and America with regard to this question had been completely safeguarded.

Eden returned to London to a very changed situation from that which he had left on 7 December 1941. Throughout that year he had continuously warned the Japanese government of the consequences of initiating war. Nevertheless, the first blow had been struck and soon the Far East was aflame. During his visit to Washington in December, Churchill secured an undertaking that the European theatre of war would have first priority. The first half of 1942 continued to be a disastrous period for the allied war effort, with Britain, Russia and the United States hard pressed all over the world. The immediate outlook was very grim, but ultimate victory was no longer in doubt.

Diplomatic relations with Britain's two powerful allies, the

United States and the Soviet Union, became Eden's main concern for the duration of the war. Relations with the Americans were not always smooth, but at least there were no basic conflicts of interest. With the USSR, however, there were major areas in dispute which, as victory came closer, became more contentious. Eden warned his colleagues at the end of January 1942 that with Germany defeated and France weakened after the war, the USSR would dominate the continent. Moreover, Soviet forces would then be deployed further west than their 1941 frontiers. He advised the War Cabinet therefore that it might be useful to satisfy Stalin's frontier demands. This calculating and quite uncharacteristic view was advanced with great hesitation. Eden was conscious, too, of Roosevelt's edict about leaving frontier questions to the post-war settlement. In the following weeks negotiations were opened with Moscow in an attempt to meet these conflicting objectives.

Vyacheslav Molotov, the tough Soviet foreign minister, arrived in London on 20 May to continue the Anglo–Soviet negotiations. Eden, with the help of his judicious permanent under-secretary, Sir Alexander Cadogan, had prepared a draft treaty which gave the USSR a twenty-year post-war alliance against German aggression instead of recognition of Stalin's frontier claims. At first the talks went badly. Molotov considered the question of the opening of a second front more important than the treaty. Churchill explained the difficulties of the second front. Eden stoutly argued the case for the British draft treaty. Suddenly, on 25 May, Molotov agreed to sign. There was general rejoicing in Downing Street. Churchill was lavish in the praise he heaped on what he regarded as a first-class piece of work by his foreign secretary. Everyone in London preferred not to think about the fact that the treaty postponed the really thorny issues to the time when the USSR would be in a better position to enforce her demands.

Churchill decided in early June to pay a second visit to Washington. Before leaving he wrote on 16 June a letter to King George VI with momentous significance for Eden's career. Churchill advised that in the event of his death the task of forming a government should be entrusted to Eden, 'who is in my mind the outstanding Minister in the largest political party in the House of Commons and in the National Government over which I have the honour to preside, and who I am sure will be found capable of conducting Your Majesty's affairs with resolution, experience, and capacity which these grievous times require'. Eden himself was hardly surprised. He recalled Churchill's assurance on 30 September 1940 that the succession would be his. This had been reiterated during an after-dinner conversation on 11 November 1941. Often during the war Churchill showed signs of fatigue, even depression. He told Eden that he did not regard himself as indispensable, that he was an old man, and that he would not make Lloyd George's mistake of carrying on after the last war. It was the central tragedy of Eden's career that he was to remain in Churchill's shadow for another thirteen years.

Eden's personal prestige and position were further enhanced in November when he took over the leadership of the House of Commons. He had been reluctant to accept the position. His time was already occupied with meetings of the War Cabinet and the Defence Committee, besides the work of the Foreign Office, often involving travel abroad. He proved to be a success, but the job, he wrote in *The Reckoning*, 'meant a ruthless burning of the candle at both ends for the better part of three years, for which excess there is always a price to be paid'.

The price that Eden was to pay included more than just the damage to his health. His marriage was eventually to prove another casualty. For the Edens were gradually drifting apart. While her husband busied himself with the politics of the war, Mrs Eden operated at the YMCA headquarters a mobile tea canteen presented by the Allied Relief Fund for service with the troops. Her good humour and friendly helpfulness commended her to everyone. Later she took over the running of the All Services Canteen in the Grand Hotel in Paris, and was for a time British director of the Allied Expeditionary Club there. It became a rare event for the Edens to be noticed spending an evening out together.

A major turn in the fortunes of the Allied powers occurred on 8 November with the launching of operation 'Torch', the landing of Allied troops in French North Africa. The successful invasion opened up possibilities of working eastwards across the North African coast, preparing for an invasion of Italy and relieving the hard-pressed eastern end. Operation 'Torch' also gave renewed impetus to begin planning the post-war settlement. That was a field that had an abiding interest for Eden throughout the war, but on which he ultimately exerted little influence. In December he told the House of Commons that after the war the United States,

the Soviet Union, Britain and China would have a virtual monopoly
of armed power. The continued maintenance of peace, however,
depended on great power unity. That strength must be exercised
for the good of all nations through the authority of a United Nations
organization. In his first Cabinet paper on the subject, in March
1943, Eden warned that failure by the victorious powers to agree
on a common policy would result in rivalry, with each power
supported by a circle of client states. It was an accurate forecast of
what happened when wartime co-operation gave way to peacetime
conflict. As to the future of Germany, Eden proved indecisive. He
favoured the disarmament of Germany, though he always opposed
the more drastic plans for dismemberment.

President Roosevelt's decision not to have his secretary of state
accompany him to the Casablanca conference in January 1943
forced Churchill, despite his wishes, to leave Eden behind. Early
in the month Roosevelt had sent Eden a message inviting him to
Washington. With the full approval of Churchill, who wished his
foreign secretary to establish personal relations with the president,
Eden arrived in Washington on 12 March for a three-week visit.
It was the first of several journeys abroad in 1943 which were to
enhance his international reputation. He had long conversations on
many topics with State Department officials and with Harry
Hopkins, the intimate adviser of the president. Eden also spent a
lot of time with Roosevelt, who described him in a telegram to
Churchill as 'a grand fellow', and stated they were 'talking everything, from Ruthenia to the production of peanuts'. Roosevelt was
in an expansive mood, and expressed surprising opinions on all
subjects. Eden, for his part, was impressed by the president's lively
mind, but seemed shocked by what he called Roosevelt's alarming
fecklessness, 'juggling with balls of dynamite'. Only later was he
reassured by Harry Hopkins that Roosevelt was engaging on one
of his tactics of trying out new ideas on a visitor. On the whole
Eden was again charmed by the president, who was in turn
impressed by Eden's knowledge of foreign affairs.

During his stay Eden's only major public engagement was to
address, at Roosevelt's suggestion, the State Legislature of Maryland in Annapolis. The occasion had an almost embarrassing
personal significance for Eden. Maryland had been originally
colonized in the seventeenth century by George Calvert, first Lord
Baltimore. Calvert's descendants included Caroline Calvert, Eden's

great-great-grandmother, who had married Sir Robert Eden, Maryland's last colonial governor and a personal friend of George Washington. The warm reception he received made Eden feel that he was an Annapolis boy who had made good.

No sooner had he returned from Washington than he was asked by Churchill to join him in Algiers. Eden had persistently worked as an honest broker for union between General Charles de Gaulle's French National Committee and the French forces in North Africa, led by General Henri Giraud. The American government was still opposed to setting up a single French authority in advance of an Allied landing. Churchill himself generally inclined to this view. A meeting between the two French generals had been arranged to take place in Algiers. Churchill had therefore invited Eden to be best man at the Giraud–de Gaulle wedding. The negotiations went well and an agreement was concluded on 3 June, without Eden's assistance, for the formation of a French Committee of National Liberation. With little in fact to do, Eden was invited to participate in Churchill's discussions with the supreme commander of Allied forces, General Dwight D. Eisenhower. Talk centred on the forthcoming invasion of Sicily and Italy, with Eden contributing to the discussion an analysis of the probable attitude of Turkey in the event that Italy was knocked out of the war. Eden then spent some time with Churchill visiting British forces and enjoying some agreeable bathing expeditions.

On their return to London, Churchill and Eden spent many hours together discussing the appointment of a new viceroy of India. Eden's own name had actually been advanced. For a brief time Churchill was receptive to the idea. For a brief moment, too, Eden grew fascinated with the prospects of being in charge of the destiny of that vast sub-continent. The prospect also of working on his own and being his own master likewise appealed to him. The deciding factor against his acceptance was the calculated realization that the Indian post meant the end of his coveted position as Churchill's successor. Finally in June Wavell was appointed viceroy.

The formation of the French Committee of National Liberation continued to present problems to both Britain and the United States. Roosevelt persisted in his suspicion of de Gaulle and refused to grant the Committee *de facto* recognition. Churchill continued to waver. But to Eden the issues involved were matters of extreme

importance for the future. The containment of Germany would be
the main post-war problem, he argued in a Cabinet paper on the
subject in early July. The Soviet Union would collaborate to this
end on Germany's eastern frontier. This had to be balanced, in the
west, by a powerful France. It appeared to Eden at the time that
Britain would end up working more closely with France in post-
war Europe than with the United States. On the more general
question of Germany, Eden was now firmly in favour of a division
of Germany, for the purposes of occupation, into three zones,
including forces from the smaller Allies under inter-Allied command. And it was this view which he formally presented on 11
August to the War Cabinet Committee on the Post-War Settlement. The Committee was in general agreement with the foreign
secretary.

Eden's relationship with Churchill in the war years has been
described by both men as one of mutual respect and harmony,
glossing over moments when they were engaged in acrimonious
debate. By the middle of July the controversy over recognition of
the French Committee threatened a permanent break between
Eden and Churchill. So fierce had Eden's support for recognition
become that he had to deny to Churchill that he was contemplating resignation on the issue. For his part, Churchill seemed to
accept a break as inevitable. The controversy, however, did not
persist and was soon to be resolved.

The successful Allied invasion of Italy on 10 July was followed
by the dramatic resignation of Mussolini and the first air raid on
Rome. Churchill was anxious for another Anglo–American meeting, and at Roosevelt's suggestion Quebec city was chosen. The
next stage in the Mediterranean campaign, and plans for the cross-
channel invasion in 1944, operation 'Overlord', were high on the
agenda. Eden joined Churchill on 18 August at the ancient citadel
in Quebec overlooking the St Lawrence River.

Eden did not participate in the main meetings between Churchill
and Roosevelt, though he was on occasion present for formal
dinners and informal discussions. He spent most of his time con-
ferring with Harry Hopkins and the secretary of state, Cordell
Hull. None of Eden's negotiating talents could persuade the
American officials to change their hostile views of the French
Committee for National Liberation. The two governments agreed
to differ. Britain granted recognition while the State Department

contented itself with a formula which accepted but did not recognize the Committee.

Talk of another meeting with the Soviet government had been current even before the Quebec conference. Stalin knew that an invasion of France had been put off until 1944. He was also disturbed about the lack of consultation with his Anglo–American allies. Eden's conversations in Quebec on the subject of relations with the USSR continued to reveal the dilemmas of the projected meeting. He was worried that he could give the Russians no assurances about the second front. More important, he realized that no progress had been made about the Soviet Union's frontier and security claims, advanced as early as 1941. A meeting in such circumstances, he told American officials, would do more harm than good.

Nevertheless, a meeting of the foreign secretaries of Britain, America and the Soviet Union opened in Moscow on 18 October. In the preceding weeks Italy had surrendered and had in turn been invaded by both the Germans from the north and the Allies from the south. On the Russian front the Red army was making substantial progress in recapturing territory lost to the Germans. But Anglo-Soviet relations were again in the doldrums due to continued controversy about the resumption of northern convoys of Allied supplies to the USSR. This conference of foreign ministers, which began with such bleak prospects, ended as one of the most successful of Allied wartime meetings.

Eden left London on 9 October and arrived in Moscow to an unusually warm reception. There followed two weeks of often contentious but ultimately fruitful negotiations. Numerous meetings with Molotov and two important sessions with Stalin produced a wide range of agreements. 'Measures to Shorten the War', or how to advance the date for operation 'Overlord', was the main topic of Soviet concern. Eden frankly explained the difficulties involved and managed to get the Soviets to accept the target date set in 1944. Likewise agreement was reached on the resumption of Arctic convoys, and the dispatch of a Soviet mission to Marshal Tito's partisans in Yugoslavia to work in contact with the British mission.

Far more important were the agreements reached for the establishment of organs of Allied co-operation: the Inter-Allied Advisory Council to deal with Italy, and the vital European Advisory

Commission to plan for the armistice and its enforcement. It was this latter body which later drew up the plans for dividing Germany into zones of occupation. Finally, the American-inspired Four Power Declaration was signed, foreshadowing the establishment of the United Nations.

The conference did not settle all issues. The problem of Polish–Soviet relations which had been broken off in April and the delimitation of Poland's post-war frontiers were hardly touched upon. Nor was the future of Germany seriously discussed. But it is not surprising that, when reporting to the House of Commons on 11 November, Eden spoke with great satisfaction about the results of the conference which had far exceeded his hopes.

Much of the credit belongs to Eden. Among his party in Moscow was Lieutenant-General Sir (later Lord) H. L. Ismay, chief of staff to the minister of defence. Ismay confessed in his memoirs that he had previously regarded Eden as 'one of fortune's darlings', whose meteoric success had been due to charming manners and a lucky flair for diplomacy. The Moscow conference changed Ismay's opinion. For he was now impressed by Eden's capacity for hard work, thoroughness, absorption with detail, and a combination of toughness and conciliation in negotiation. Likewise the American secretary of state, Cordell Hull, for the first time seemed to have come to an appreciation of Eden's qualities of co-operation and broadmindedness.

Among Eden's achievements in Moscow were arrangements for a meeting of the 'Big Three' at Tehcran. That conference was preceded by a meeting, mainly on Far Eastern military topics, between Churchill, Roosevelt and General Chiang Kai-shek at Cairo. Eden was becoming more and more concerned, as victory approached, with the post-war shape of Europe. The delimitation of Polish–Soviet frontiers, the future of Greece, where civil war now raged, and of Yugoslavia, where resistance movements flourished, beside the perennial problem of how to administer occupied Germany, were all issues which needed decisive action. The preliminary meeting at Cairo, where Eden arrived on 24 November, provided him with little guidance and afforded scant progress. He drew some consolation from his first meeting with the Chinese leader and American protégé, General Chiang Kai-shek, whose qualities he grew to admire.

Teheran provided Roosevelt with his first meeting and long-awaited opportunity to discuss global strategy with Joseph Stalin. Churchill felt overshadowed by what he called the great Russian bear on one side and the great American buffalo on the other. Naturally, Eden was overshadowed by all three, although he concentrated on several vital issues where he sought guidelines for the future. Churchill raised with Stalin, in Eden's presence, the vexed question of Poland. Stalin stated that Poland's western frontiers should be on the Oder river. Churchill liked this idea of moving Poland's frontiers westwards, which he 'demonstrated with the help of three matches'. Two days later Stalin asked for the Curzon Line of 1920 as Poland's eastern frontier. Subsequent conversation, in which Eden participated, revealed differences of opinion as to where this line should be drawn on the map. Eden pointed out that, with some minor variation, the Curzon Line had been the boundary between the German and Soviet spheres of occupation after the Nazi–Soviet pact of August 1939. 'I began to fear greatly for the Poles', Eden noted in *The Reckoning*. As far as Stalin's ideas on the post-war government of the world, it is interesting to note that they resembled closely ideas on the subject which Eden had propounded in December 1942. For Stalin disliked, as Eden had, Roosevelt's scheme of the 'Four Policemen', the United States, Britain, the USSR, and China, supervising the general peace. It was at this meeting that Eden began also to be disturbed, because of sudden shifts in Soviet policy, about future collaboration with the USSR.

Eden was on the whole a passive witness to the major strategic decisions reached at Teheran. The results, he told the House of Commons on 14 December after his return to London, would soon be 'unrolled on the fields of battle'. He then declared in an outburst of optimism that the Moscow and Teheran conferences had laid the foundations for co-operation between the three great powers to reshape post-war Europe along peaceful lines. As he spoke he reminded members that it was 'the heart of the fifth winter of this war'. It was also the first winter of real hope. As 1944 opened the Red army continued to attack victoriously. The Allied advance in Italy was being held before Monte Cassino, but major progress had been made. While in the Far East the tide of war was beginning to flow against the Japanese.

The months of waiting for the momentous Allied invasion of France meanwhile provided Eden with various problems to un-

ravel. As Soviet forces re-entered Poland in the first week of the
new year, he did his best to smooth Soviet–Polish relations. He did
not want 'to throw the poor Poles to the Russian wolves', although
he realized sadly that Britain did not have the power or influence
to exert pressure on the Russians for moderation either in frontier
demands or policy towards the Poles. This sadness was further
tinged with bitterness. It was after all the decision to assist Poland
which had brought Britain into World War II. It was during these
weeks, too, and still with the Polish problem as his chief preoccupation, that Eden posed the question which was to dominate
all others as victory neared: 'Is the Soviet regime one which will
ever co-operate with the West?' He confessed to a growing apprehension, as he noted in *The Reckoning*, 'that Russia has vast aims
and that these may include the domination of Eastern Europe and
even the Mediterranean and the "communising" of much that
remains'. Speaking on 28 March to a meeting of the Free Church
Federal Council, he hinted that the British government could not
at all times and in all places impose her judgment on others.
Nevertheless, he reiterated a conviction which has always been
associated with his career: the principle of moral purpose in international relations. He quoted with obvious approval the words of
the American statesman John Quincy Adams: 'The more of pure
moral principle that is carried into the policy of a Government, the
wiser and more profound will that policy be.' Eden's career
abundantly illustrated both the strength and weakness of these
words.

Much of Eden's time was spent trying to bring some semblance
of order into the complicated affairs of Yugoslavia and Greece. In
both countries short-term military expediency had forced support
for left-wing resistance movements at the expense of long-term
political interests. Fear was growing in the Foreign Office about
the spread of Soviet influence throughout the Balkans. It was
Eden's view that this penetration could not be resisted but only
contained by a consolidation of British interests in Greece and
Turkey. Finally these winter months provided an opportunity for
work to progress on a project for a post-war regional council for
Europe and on draft schemes for the future United Nations organization. The physical effort exerted by Eden in combining leadership of the House of Commons and the Foreign Office forced him
to take a rest in April. He discussed with Churchill the possibility

of appointing a new foreign secretary. But such talk, a symptom of almost five years' war weariness, was short-lived.

On 6 June, D-Day for operation 'Overlord', Eden was in London, deeply involved in French problems. For weeks he had made prodigious efforts to smooth the transition period towards a civil administration in a liberated France. He argued vehemently against Churchill and Roosevelt's refusal to grant this authority to de Gaulle and the French Committee for National Liberation. Eden was determined not to give way. A meeting he had arranged between himself, Churchill and de Gaulle, invited back to London on the eve of 'Overlord', was a complete failure. De Gaulle refused to assist in managing the civil affairs of France until an official agreement with both Britain and America had been negotiated. A solution eventually emerged, not in London, but in France where the resistance movement acknowledged de Gaulle as its leader.

The Allied advance into France continued throughout June and July, while in eastern Europe the Red army captured Lublin, west of the Curzon Line. A Polish Committee of National Liberation, the puppet Lublin Committee, was encouraged by Stalin to set up a civil administration. In the middle of August, while Churchill was in Italy witnessing the preparations for the major offensive against the Gothic Line north of Florence, Eden paid a brief visit to France. Inevitably the sights brought back to him memories of his own experiences in World War I. Eden was in charge of the government for a few days before Churchill's return to London and was no doubt pleased to be able to sign the final agreement, made possible by Roosevelt's sudden change of mind, to recognize the French Committee as the *de facto* civil authority in France. Its recognition as a provisional government followed in October.

In early September Churchill and Roosevelt held their second conference in Quebec city to discuss the progress made in Europe and the next stages of the offensive in the Far East. Eden, at Churchill's specific request, joined the conference for four days. Most of his time was spent hanging about. His only major contribution, and one which brought him into sharp conflict with Churchill, was to pour cold water on the Morgenthau plan to 'pastoralize' Germany after the war. This was the only occasion when Churchill ever displayed impatience with Eden's view before foreign representatives.

Continued anxiety about the future of Poland and the threat of Soviet penetration into the Balkans prompted Churchill and Eden to visit Moscow on 9 October for ten days. The atmosphere was generally relaxed, and Churchill was convinced that the time was propitious for business. For the purposes of the war and simply as a guide to the conduct of Balkan affairs, Churchill and Stalin agreed on a division of interest in south-east Europe. For his part, Eden severely reproached Molotov for the policy of self-interest which the Soviet government was pursuing in the Balkan states.

Churchill had cajoled Stalin into receiving members of the London Polish government in exile, who now joined the Moscow conference. Eden tried his best, however unsuccessfully, to present the issues of Poland as best left to the Poles to decide. Churchill on the contrary took a very hard line with the London Poles. He pressed them, also unsuccessfully, to accept the Curzon Line and engage in practical discussions with the Lublin Committee on the formation of a government. Both men formed the most critical opinion of the Soviet-supported Poles. 'They seemed creepy to me', was Eden's blunt assessment.

The controversial topic of Germany's future was only briefly discussed in Moscow. Stalin stated that he still favoured a policy of dismemberment. Eden had to reply weakly that the British government had not as yet come to a definite conclusion on the subject. In his own mind he now feared that dismemberment would allow Stalin unlimited opportunities for expansion in a weakened and divided Europe. The visit was climaxed with the usual lavish performance at the Bolshoi Theatre. For Churchill, if not Eden, the conference marked the apex of Anglo–Soviet collaboration as wartime allies.

Eden broke his homeward flight for a round of visits in the Mediterranean area. He had anticipated visiting the British army in Italy. Instead, he was urgently asked by the British ambassador in Greece to hurry directly to Athens. The liberation of Greece, where British troops had landed on 4 October, had brought with it political and economic dislocation. Rampant inflation combined with an unsettled internal political situation was giving cause for alarm. Eden was out of his depth in tackling the economic situation and wired to London for a Treasury adviser, whose arrival quickly helped to stabilize the situation. The political situation, however, was more intractable, and Eden feared the outbreak of a civil war between the royalist Government of National Unity and the communist-inspired ELAS, the National Army of Liberation.

No sooner had Eden returned to London than he was accompanying Churchill to participate in the memorable Armistice Day celebrations in Paris on 11 November. The visit added momentum to discussions which had been proceeding for some time in London with regard to the formation of a western European bloc. Churchill was lukewarm towards the project, preferring, as he told the Cabinet on 27 November, to rely on continued agreement with the three great powers within the framework of a world organization. Eden, in contrast, drew what to him was the obvious lesson of the disaster of 1940: the need to build a common defence organization in western Europe. Thus it was vital again to strengthen the French, who together with the smaller western European states would then have an impregnable system of defence in depth. For the meantime no conclusion was reached on this subject.

For the second time in the war Eden was destined to play a controversial role in Greek affairs. In early December civil war broke out in Athens. On the 5th Churchill and Eden, without Cabinet authority, ordered the British commander in Greece, Lieutenant-General Ronald Scobie, to use his forces against the ELAS rebels. Eden was forced to defend this decision in the House of Commons twice. He carefully revealed the facts regarding his long attempts to bring unity to the divided Greek nation. His speeches, among his best ever in the House, quelled criticism that the government had interfered in the internal affairs of an allied country in support of reactionary forces.

Fierce fighting continued meanwhile in Athens. Eden put his full authority, both within the Cabinet and outside, in support of the idea of appointing a regent to take charge of Greek affairs and form a new government. Churchill disliked the idea and quarrelled with Eden, whose inclinations were to visit Athens. On Christmas eve it was both who made a dramatic descent on the Greek capital, determined to force an end to the civil war. A conference of interested parties, including ELAS, was hastily arranged. The prime minister and foreign secretary were driven through the darkened streets in an armoured car to the meeting. A face to face encounter with the projected regent converted Churchill to the Eden solution and it was endorsed by all parties. An armistice was agreed and a new government was formed early in the new year. On 19 January a parliamentary vote of confidence confirmed the success of the British intervention.

The Greek civil war was only one of the many symptoms of the increasingly heavy hand of the USSR unsettling the wartime alliance. Despite protests from Churchill and Roosevelt, re-elected as president, Stalin recognized on 5 January 1945 the Lublin Committee as the provisional government of Poland. This upset seemed symbolic of the diplomatic troubles casting their shadow over military victories. Another meeting of the wartime leaders was necessary. Eden had witnessed enough of these conferences to convince him that careful preparation was needed to ensure an orderly dispatch of business. Otherwise Stalin, who always had a clear notion of his priorities, was bound to triumph. Eden pressed Churchill, therefore, to sanction a preliminary meeting of foreign secretaries. There were numerous questions on which the prime minister and particularly Roosevelt were still reluctant to make a definite decision. Finally, Eden advised Churchill not to accede to any Soviet demands without reciprocal concessions. Such advice was easier to give than to follow.

The foreign secretaries' conference never materialized. Instead, Eden joined Churchill at the end of January for a meeting on Malta with the Americans. No official business was transacted, much to Eden's annoyance and dismay. The Anglo–American party then journeyed to the Crimea. The last wartime meeting of the 'Big Three' took place at Yalta from 4 to 11 February. The Anglo–American alliance was already showing signs of strain, which profited the Soviet Union in the diplomatic spoils game acted out at Yalta. In *The Reckoning* Eden was critical of both Roosevelt, whom he regarded as lacking in long-range vision, and of Churchill, whose qualities of generosity, impulsiveness and loquacity proved a handicap at the negotiating table. As for Stalin, Eden was confirmed in his undiluted admiration for him as the toughest negotiator he had ever met.

The format of the Yalta conference, with the foreign secretaries meeting each morning, provided Eden with a full schedule of work. As a result he left his mark on the conference. He succeeded in getting Stalin to agree to withdraw Soviet troops from Iran. He successfully contested the Soviet suggestion to dismember Germany. Zones of occupation were allocated instead. And in the final stages, he openly quarrelled with Churchill's desire to join in the signature of an agreement secretly signed between Roosevelt and Stalin about the Far East war. Not unexpectedly, Churchill went ahead.

It was the subject of Poland, discussed at almost every session of the conference, which passionately occupied Eden. With support from the new American secretary of state, Edward Stettinius, Eden insisted that the solution lay in the creation of a new provisional government of both Lublin and London Poles pledged to hold free elections. This was accepted by Stalin. But no agreement could be reached with regard to Poland's western frontier. The acceptance of the Curzon Line in the east meant compensation for the Poles in the west at German expense. A definite delineation there was deferred to a final peace conference. The Polish issue, like other contentious matters between the 'Big Three', rested upon good faith. Churchill at the time exuded both publicly and in the Cabinet the utmost trust in Stalin's intentions. It was, however, as Eden pointed out in *The Reckoning*, 'the execution which mattered'.

After a visit to Athens, where he surveyed progress since Christmas, Eden returned to London. The atmosphere was quickly darkening. Against strong and often emotional criticism Eden defended the Yalta agreements regarding Poland in a Commons debate at the end of February. He spoke with little conviction and hardly a hint of his anxieties regarding Soviet intentions, which he reserved for the privacy of the Cabinet. Arrangements made at Yalta to reorganize the Lublin government soon broke down. In early March Romania was brought into the Soviet orbit. Yugoslavia appeared to be threatened next, while Turkey was suddenly subjected to unwarranted Soviet pressure. 'I take the gloomiest view of Russian behaviour everywhere', Eden noted in his diary on 23 March. 'Altogether our foreign policy seems a sad wreck and we may have to cast about afresh.'

It was against this background of deteriorating relations with the USSR that Eden left for the San Francisco conference, arranged to set up the United Nations Organization. He arrived in Washington in time to attend the funeral of President Roosevelt, who had died on 12 April, and to meet his successor, Harry Truman. The latter impressed Eden as 'honest and friendly'. The conference opened on 25 April and was addressed by Eden the next day. He expressed his hopes in the future of the UN despite previous failures of international peace-keeping organizations. The responsibilities of the

ABOVE Robert Anthony Eden with his mother.

LEFT Lieutenant R. A. Eden returning from Buckingham Palace after his investiture with the Military Cross, 1917.

ABOVE Eden and Sir John Simon in Berlin for talks with Hitler, 25 March 1935.

BELOW Eden addressing the League of Nations, October 1935.

ABOVE 19 February 1938; a crowd gathers in Downing Street as Eden arrives for an emergency cabinet meeting where he will announce his resignation.

BELOW Chamberlain's War Cabinet, November 1939. Standing, from left to right: Sir John Anderson (minister of home security); Lord Hankey (minister without portfolio); Leslie Hore-Belisha (secretary of state for war); Winston Churchill (first lord of the Admiralty); Sir Kingsley Wood (secretary of state for air); Eden (secretary of state for dominion affairs); Sir Edward Bridges (secretary to the War Cabinet). Seated: Viscount Halifax (secretary of state for foreign affairs); Sir John Simon (chancellor of the exchequer); Chamberlain; Sir Samuel Hoare (lord privy seal); Lord Chatfield (minister for the co-ordination of defence).

ABOVE LEFT In Churchill's shoes at last; Eden and Churchill on the steps of No. 10 shortly after Eden took over the premiership.
ABOVE RIGHT Eden and Nikita Khrushchev meet for talks in London, April 1956.
BELOW The Western 'Big Three'; Christian Pineau, the French foreign minister, Eden and John Foster Dulles, the US secretary of state, emerge from private talks at No. 10.

ABOVE Campaigning
for the first time as
prime minister, Eden
addresses a meeting at
Uxbridge a few days
before the election,
May 1955.

LEFT Attending to
domestic affairs; Eden
dons overalls and
helmet to inspect a
huge reconstruction
scheme at the
Woodhorn Colliery,
Northumberland,
September 1955.

ABOVE Eden's first and only meeting with Gamal Abdel Nasser, in February 1955, was on the whole a friendly affair.

ɅILY **2d**

SKETCH

THURSDAY, AUGUST 9. 1956

Blunt, stern Eden: This act of plunder must not succeed

A MATTER OF LIFE AND DEATH

Britain's resolve to keep the Canal free has not weakened

SIR ANTHONY EDEN, in one of the most critical broadcasts of his career, last night warned the world: Nasser's Suez Canal grab is a matter of life and death to us all in Britain.

Millions of viewers and listeners heard him declare bluntly: " We do not seek a solution by force, but there can be no appeasement."

Speaking slowly and deliberately, emphasising each word, he said: " I must make it plain we cannot agree that an act of plunder which threatens the life of many nations will be allowed to succeed."

The Prime Minister made it clear Britain's quarrel is not with Egypt or with the Arab world.

" It is with Colonel Nasser," he declared. " He has shown he is not a man who can be trusted to keep an agreement.

" Now he has torn up all his country's promises towards the Suez Canal Company.

" He has even gone back on his own statement."

Dramatically, he labelled Nasser's tactics as Fascist. " We all remember only too well what the cost can be of giving in to Fascism."

Sir Anthony said the Suez Canal was a lifeline to the West—it must be run in the interests of all.

WEALTH FOR ALL

" We must make sure the lives of the great trading nations of the world cannot, in future, be strangled at any moment by some interruption of the free passage of the Canal.

The Canal must be kept open as a free and secure international waterway.

" In our view this can only be secured by an international body," Sir Anthony said.

" There will be wealth ⇨ *Back Page*

❝ If Colonel Nasser's action were to succeed each one of us would be at the mercy of one man for the supplies on which we live. We could never accept that **❞**

Early in 1956 the British Press was already expressing discontent with Eden's leadership. His alleged indecision and half-measures drew criticism from all quarters not least from the cartoonist Vicky (left). Initially the Press supported Eden's firm stand over Suez – (above) the *Daily Sketch* reports his broadcast to the nation, 9 August – but his subsequent policies left Fleet Street deeply divided.

A tired and ill man, Eden leaves No. 10 for Buckingham Palace to offer his resignation to the Queen, 9 January 1957.

great powers, he pointedly added, remained to allow all nations to develop a free and independent life. His words expressed a brave and pious hope in a world already returning to power politics. The charter of the United Nations, signed on 25 June, recognized the fundamental reality that peace could only be preserved by great power harmony.

While Eden enjoyed the attention of photographers and auto-graph hunters who followed him everywhere in San Francisco, World War II was drawing to a close. He celebrated the uncon-ditional surrender of Germany on 7 May with a dinner party for the commonwealth prime ministers. The end of the war presaged the winding up of the wartime coalition government. In early May Eden had opposed deferring an election until the autumn, fearing that the international situation would by then have deteriorated. The Labour party, too, opted for a return to party politics. Churchill announced on 23 May that a general election would take place on 5 July and that the affairs of the nations would meanwhile be managed by a caretaker government.

Eden had returned to London on 17 May, to be plunged immediately into planning the election. He did not take to it easily, having none of what he called Churchill's 'lust for electoral battle . There was also too much generosity in his nature to begin taking to task colleagues with whom he had worked for five years. Finally, he was troubled by a personal disillusionment with party politics. In the latter stages of the war he had confessed in his diary that he, like so many others, had no real party politics. How then, he asked, was an election to express the welter of emotions stirred by war? To one question at least he now had an answer. Despite indications to the contrary, Churchill intended to continue as the leader of the party and, in case of victory, as prime minister.

On his return from San Francisco Eden paid the price of almost five years' overwork. He had always been a prodigious worker, exacting, well-prepared and meticulous. The continued demands of conference diplomacy, the Foreign Office and leading the House affected his health. A duodenal ulcer was diagnosed and he re-treated to his country home where he spent almost the entire campaign. His misery was heightened by domestic tragedy. On 17 June his mother, Lady Sybil Eden, died at Windlestone at the age of seventy-eight. He had been devoted to her and, through the years, had kept her abreast of all his activities. Already in February

1943 his sister Marjorie, Countess of Warwick, had died. She had twice been mayoress of Warwick and her villa in the south of France had before the war been a welcome retreat for Eden. In June 1945, too, Eden received news that his twenty-one year old son Simon, who had trained as a pilot under the Commonwealth Air Training Scheme in Canada, was reported missing in Burma. Simon's final leave in London, during December 1944, had been marred by his father's sudden visit to Athens. In July Eden received confirmation of Simon's death.

Party election strife replaced wartime harmony with astonishing speed. Churchill assumed, wrongly, that his reputation as wartime leader would carry him to victory. The Labour party appealed less dramatically to the nation on a programme of wide-ranging social reform. Although Beatrice Eden dutifully, if also half-heartedly, electioneered on her husband's behalf, Eden was able to make one election broadcast on 27 June. Its main purpose was to appeal for continuity in Britain's foreign relations.

The speech contained an imaginative appeal to the younger voters and servicemen, whose dislike of 'the old party war cries' Eden professed he understood. The performance was in a low key, with distinct undertones that the speaker somehow lacked conviction on the prospects for election victory.

On 15 July Churchill, Eden, and Attlee, invited to ensure continuity whatever the election results, left for the Potsdam conference. Poland was again the subject of some of the toughest discussions with Stalin. On 5 July the British and United States Governments had finally recognized the Lublin Committee, now constituted as the Warsaw government, with some Cabinet places given to Poles from abroad. The Polish government in London was disbanded. Eden reluctantly acquiesced in this procedure, remembering the Yalta decision on free elections for Poland.

At Potsdam no agreement was reached on the controversial issue of Poland's western frontier. Eden pressed for the line of the Oder and eastern Neisse rivers, fearing that too large a Germany would weaken the future Polish state. The conference eventually agreed to a provisional occupation up to the western Neisse. Throughout the deliberations he urged Churchill to take a strong line and use the few bargaining counters still left, such as the disposal of the German fleet and Stalin's wish for access to the eastern Mediterranean. But at every point he found the prime minister 'again under Stalin's spell'. Ultimately more momentous was the secret of the successful explosion of an atomic bomb, which Eden urged should be revealed to Stalin during the course of the conference. The British delegation had then agreed to the use of this weapon against Japan. On 14 August, after the atomic bombings of Hiroshima and Nagasaki, the surrender of Japan ended the war in the Far East and with it World War II.

On 25 July Eden returned home to await the election results, due the following day. At Warwick he heard the welcome news that he had retained his seat with a majority of 17,634 votes. It proved to be among the largest Conservative majorities in the country. After a tour of his constituency he began a depressing drive through the rain back to London. For during the day it had become clear that the Conservative party had suffered an election disaster. The results, the first test of national opinion since 1935, showed an overwhelming majority for the Labour party with 393 members. The Conservatives had 213 seats, less than half their 1935 total, and Churchill resigned. In his diary Eden wrote that day: 'It was foolish to try to win on Winston's personality alone instead of on a programme.'

At noon on 27 July Churchill held his farewell Cabinet. Afterwards he and Eden stayed behind to console each other. 'Thirty years of my life have been passed in this room', the prime minister said. 'I shall never sit in it again. You will, but I shall not.' Eden made no comment.

4
OPPOSITION AND OFFICE
1945-1955

PARLIAMENTARY opposition held little attraction for Anthony Eden. He was appointed foreign affairs spokesman in the shadow Cabinet and like most of his colleagues had his first experience of the opposition front bench. The domestic politics of the Labour government concerned with building the welfare state were beyond Eden's immediate range of competence, although he was soon to remedy this deficiency. Foreign affairs naturally continued to absorb him. It was not within his character nor did he wish to make that subject a party political issue. Moreover, he had during the war grown to like and admire the new Labour foreign secretary, Ernest Bevin, even to the extent of canvassing unofficially for his appointment to the Foreign Office.

There proved to be little in Bevin's policies during the next five years which Eden could not support. The basic reality of Soviet and American power, support for collective security and the rule of law as exercised through the United Nations, and colonial emancipation, were concepts as acceptable to Eden as to Bevin. Likewise Bevin's framework incorporating the acceptance of United States' leadership in world affairs, the restoration of France's position as a major power in western Europe, and the commitment to the world-wide defence of western interests was a course Eden had no cause to contest.

The first parliamentary debate on foreign affairs in which Eden spoke, on 20 August 1945, from the opposition benches, found him in a complimentary mood. He acknowledged Bevin's valuable role in the coalition government and looked forward to parliament functioning as a sort of Council of State on foreign affairs. It was clear that there would be no partisan zeal emanating from Eden. Furthermore, with Bevin's approval, he was to be kept informed and supplied with Foreign Office telegrams throughout Bevin's tenure of office.

Eden's popularity, in spite of the Conservative party's massive defeat, survived undiminished. And he still remained Churchill's chosen successor. But defeat at the polls had inaugurated a period of profound re-examination within the Conservative party. If Labour policies had triumphed over Tory personalities the deficiency had to be overcome. A new chairman of the party, Lord Woolton, who had served as food minister during the war, began an immediate overhaul of its organization. R. A. Butler became the leading figure in the research department, charged with framing new policies and giving the Conservatives a permanent face-lift. Eden himself made a significant contribution to this process and chaired many of the committees working on new plans and manifestoes. But his contribution was limited by other duties. Winston Churchill pursued his numerous interests, frequently leaving Eden to preside over weekly meetings in the House of Commons to discuss parliamentary business, and sometimes even to chair the shadow Cabinet.

Eden had never been a wealthy man, although he had a comfortable private income. During the war he had been overspending by almost £1000 a year. The burden of maintaining an elegant style of life and keeping up his London and country homes forced him to seek additional income. In October 1945 he accepted a directorship of the Westminster Bank. The chairman was Rupert Beckett, the brother of Eden's father-in-law, Sir Gervase Beckett, whose family bank had been absorbed by the Westminster. A year later Eden was to join the boards of the Rio Tinto group and the Phoenix Assurance Company. These were his first ventures into the commercial field, a natural temptation for members of parliament, but one which he had long resisted. In the autumn of 1945 he was also installed as chancellor of Birmingham University and made a freeman of Durham. The freedom of Warwick was to follow in June 1947.

Just before Christmas it was announced that Churchill would

spend several months on holiday in the United States. In his absence Eden led the opposition during the important debates in January 1946 against the Labour government's coal nationalization bill. His speech was not a fighting lead against the principles of state nationalization. Instead, he asked whether the bill embodied the nationalization ideas the miners themselves wished, and he criticized the future organization of the bill as outlined by the government.

In reply to a general demand among Conservative voters for a statement of policy in answer to Labour's seeming monopoly on domestic issues, Eden made the first of several pronouncements on the subject. It had never been his strong point, although it would be wrong to underrate his interest and grasp of the issues. He now began to make a special effort to broaden his competence in this field. Speaking at Hull in early March, he outlined Conservative policies to deal with the grave economic situation faced by the country. He advocated such short-term measures as increasing both consumer demand and industrial productivity, and reducing income tax. In his statement of long-term measures he revealed that he still stood among the moderate elements of the party. Conservatism, he declared, was 'neither a watered-down form of Socialism, nor is it a doctrinaire opposition to Socialism'. The function of the state was to give the fullest scope to the free development of the individual. This meant achieving a balance between the organizing power of the state and the drive of free enterprise.

Ever since the Potsdam conference Eden had anxiously watched the growing rift in the wartime grand alliance and the tightening grip of Soviet power on eastern Europe. He had no solutions to offer Bevin. But from his long experience of negotiating with the USSR Eden drew for the Commons in February a sober lesson. It was unacceptable, he stated, that Moscow should repeat its wish for unity 'as a sort of abracadabra' and then pursue a policy of non-co-operation. Later in September he pleaded for a return to confidence and a removal of suspicion. For nothing was more dangerous, he pointed out, than the situation where suspicions 'harden into facts, and these facts in their turn breed new suspicions and so the circle widens'. On both occasions his suggestions for action included closer western European unity, internationalization of the Ruhr, and a conference of commonwealth prime ministers. His final plea enshrined the basic Eden code for inter-national relations: observance of the rule of law.

In May the House of Commons was forced to debate the growing tension with Egypt, where demands had arisen for the withdrawal of troops to the Suez canal zone and the renegotiation of the Anglo–Egyptian treaty of 1936. As the minister responsible for that treaty Eden strongly defended it on 7 May against charges that it was 'derogatory' to Egyptian sovereignty. He advised the government to withdraw British forces from Cairo, which they had defended during the war, and negotiate a new arrangement with Egypt if that was the general desire. As to the future of the canal zone Eden was and remained convinced that its unique strategic position was at the same time 'an Egyptian interest and a British Imperial interest'. That was a view which was eventually to cost him his premiership. British troops were soon withdrawn to the canal zone, but no progress was made in renegotiating the treaty.

For a short time Eden turned his back on opposition duties, and in June went to Bermuda. There he attended a conference of the Empire Parliamentary Association. Afterwards he visited the United States and Canada, where prime minister Mackenzie King referred to him as 'No. 1 Goodwill Ambassador'. Return to London meant plunging again into controversies about the housing short-age, the introduction of bread rationing, and Labour measures for bills on a national health service, a national insurance scheme, and a plan to nationalize the steel industry. Eden added his voice to the rising tide of Conservative criticism. He was more outspoken this time in his attack on nationalization, if hardly more eloquent. He dismissed it as 'crazy', although he did outline some constructive aids to industry which he thought the government ought to foster instead of nationalization.

The Conservative party conference at Blackpool in October provided Eden with his widest platform for publicizing his views on domestic affairs. In a generally acclaimed speech he returned to a subject which had first appealed to him in 1930 as a young MP. He declared his fundamental belief that in the concept of owner-ship man achieved mastery over his environment. Whereas the object of socialism was state ownership, he said, 'our objective is a nation-wide property-owning democracy.' He then outlined how he expected this wider distribution of ownership to be achieved, adding a plea for partnership between government, capital and labour, and a suggestion that schemes for co-partnership in industry, with employee participation in profits, should be studied.

At Christmas Eden, his wife, and son Nicholas sailed for the United States. This proved to be the final chapter of the Edens' marriage, for after the voyage they separated. The marriage had suffered the strains imposed by Eden's political career: the constant foreign travel, the long hours, and the glare of publicity for a popular figure, who cannot be said to have shunned publicity or to have been unmoved by it. Their marriage was finally dissolved in 1950 and Beatrice Eden died seven years later.

The severe winter of 1946–7 coincided with a fuel shortage which affected industry and private users. On 20 March Eden delivered a party political broadcast on the crisis. His basic advice was that the Labour government should 'stop galloping down nationalization avenue'. As part of its fundamental reassessment programme the Conservative party published in May its *Industrial Charter*. It was approved beforehand by both Churchill and Eden. On 17 May Eden spoke at Cardiff to welcome the report. In essence it elaborated almost all that he had been discussing in committees and publicly stating about nationalization, industrial relations, and the intention of Conservatism to maintain central guidance over the management of the economy.

The winter fuel crisis was followed in the summer by an economic crisis. Imports rose, exports fell, and the government had to draw heavily on a large dollar loan negotiated the previous autumn in Washington. In early August parliament debated a series of emergency measures announced by the government. Eden wound up the debate for the opposition. He chided the government for having stumbled unprepared into the crisis, and observed that too much at one time was being done with limited resources. It could hardly have been clear to him that he was speaking during the first of many financial crises. They were to have the most far-reaching effects on all aspects of British life, not least, as Eden was later to discover, on the conduct of foreign policy. The defence of the pound was to become as important as the defence of Britain's frontiers.

European problems were again drawing America into the affairs of a continent from which she had hoped to retreat after the war. The iron curtain which now cut off all of eastern Europe and the dangers of communist subversion had to be confronted with a prosperous and united western Europe. On 5 June the American secretary of state, General George C. Marshall, announced a programme of economic aid for Europe, providing prior agreement was reached on definite plans for reconstruction. Eden gave his enthusiastic support to that already extended by Bevin. He furthermore looked forward to Marshall Aid as providing the impetus towards closer co-operation in western Europe, which he had advocated since 1945. Sixteen European nations, excluding the USSR and its satellites, agreed during the summer on a plan for European economic recovery in response to Marshall's offer. Eden welcomed this development, and he renewed in the autumn his call for western European co-operation.

During the Christmas parliamentary recess Eden left for a trip to the Middle East, accompanied by his son, Nicholas. In Iran he was received in semi-state and entertained by numerous receptions. When inspecting the Anglo–Iranian oilfields he made an impressive display of his fluency in Persian. He also visited Bahrein, where he was royally entertained, and then went on to Saudi Arabia. There he was presented by King Ibn Saud with a jewel-encrusted sword. The contacts Eden made on this trip proved invaluable when in 1951 the Anglo–Iranian Oil Company concession was terminated and its installations nationalized.

On his return to London in January 1948 Eden was pleased to hear of the enormous progress made by Bevin in the cause of European union, which he warmly welcomed in parliament. The Labour foreign minister had set in motion negotiations which on 17 March ended in the signature of the Brussels pact. It provided for military, economic and cultural co-operation between Britain, France and the Benelux countries of Belgium, Holland and Luxembourg.

In March Eden was ill again, entering a nursing home in London for the removal of his appendix, followed by three weeks' convalescence in the country. His health revived rumours about his fitness for office which had first arisen after his resignation in 1938. But he soon returned to normal political activity. On 5 May he contributed to a House of Commons foreign affairs debate. Almost a year before he had in the House denounced the 'cynicism' which had flagrantly denied the Yalta agreement on free elections in liberated countries. And abandoning his previously guarded words on the Soviet Union, he admitted that confidence and good relations had been undermined. Returning now to the subject, he deplored the debasement of the rule of law among nations and maintained that negotiations with the USSR could only be conducted from a basis of strength. He advocated, therefore, a co-ordinated military policy in western Europe, while at the same time praising Bevin's progress in the more general field of western union. Finally, worried, as was most of the Conservative party with the pace of Labour's policy of colonial emancipation, Eden asked that the commonwealth be kept informed of developments.

As an example of Soviet methods, Eden had referred to the communist coup d'état in February which brought Czechoslovakia into the Soviet orbit. At the same time in Berlin the Soviet authorities were harassing the work of the Allied Control Commission which was responsible for administering occupied Germany. Eden warned parliament against pursuing a policy of 'weak appeasement'. On 30 June, after the Soviets had imposed a complete blockade of Berlin, Eden initiated a debate in the Commons on the beleaguered city. Bevin had already declared that Britain was there as a right and intended to stay. It was the sort of crisis where Eden adopted a principled position, refusing to give in to what he regarded as brute force and blackmail. He repeated, as he was to do in later years, the lesson that he had learned from his experiences in the thirties: 'any vacillation on our part now would only encourage the rulers of the Soviet Union to believe that further pressure will result in further yielding, until at last a stand has to be taken which makes war inevitable.' The Berlin blockade was finally lifted in May 1949. By that time it had served to consolidate western defensive interests and led to the formation of the military alliance of the North Atlantic Treaty Organization (NATO).

The leisure of opposition allowed Eden the time to formulate some generalizations which he revealed to the Conservative party conference in early October and to which he reverted during the 1950 election. He called for a foreign policy based on 'three unities': unity within the commonwealth and empire; unity with western Europe; and unity across the Atlantic with the United States. It was a brave statement of an interlocking system which Eden hoped would ensure that elusive period of peace and security. It rested, however, on the assumption, later disproved, that the interests of these three unities would always coincide.

Although Eden had often spoken of the need for western European unity, his working conception of the idea had definite limitations. He had, for example, never taken part in the United Europe Movement, though he did attend its historic meeting at the Hague in May 1948. On the whole he preferred to keep himself aloof. Writing in January 1949, he hinted that he was not entirely in favour of an outright European federation, nor did he think it realizable. He remained as anxious as ever that Germany, whose three occupation zones had already been merged by the western Allies, should take its rightful place in Europe. But out of the European Movement there was finally established in May 1949 the Council of Europe at Strasbourg. Owing largely to British reservations, its functions were severely restricted.

Early in 1949 Eden left on a world tour, revisiting many of the places he had seen on his empire trip in 1925. First he travelled to Canada where on 24 January he addressed the Toronto Board of Trade. He spoke for the first time in the tones and phraseology of the cold war, condemning Soviet expansionism and exhorting the commonwealth to join in bolstering the non-communist world. He then went on to New Zealand, visiting Wellington and Auckland, the latter named after his ancestor George Eden, first Earl of Auckland. Here Eden pledged that Britain would never make any foreign agreement which cut across commonwealth interests. After touring Australia, he travelled to India as a guest of the governor-general. He had useful talks with the prime minister, Jawaharlal Nehru, and addressed the Indian parliament. With the benefit of this first-hand knowledge of the country and its leaders, he seemed to have overcome his original grudging acquiescence to the transfer of power in India. His dominant impression of his mammoth journey, he said in a broadcast from London on 27 April, had been 'underlying unity'.

While addressing a United Nations Association meeting in June, Eden suddenly collapsed. The seeds of illness were sown which were to incapacitate him on and off from 1951 to 1955, and which were to have such disastrous consequences during his premiership. By July he was with his constituents at Stoneleigh Abbey to celebrate his twenty-five years as MP for Warwick and Leamington. July, too, saw the publication of the most comprehensive of Conservative charters, *Right Road for Britain*. It was the result of work done by a committee which Eden chaired and was the basis of the party manifesto for the next election. As previously, Eden identified himself with its appearance. On 23 July he delivered a party political broadcast, pointing out that Britain was living beyond its means and promising that a Conservative government would reduce both government expenditure and taxation. Free enterprise would be 'humanized and not nationalized', with schemes for profit sharing, promotion by merit, and co-partnership. He ended with another of his trinities: 'faith, freedom and responsibility'.

The Labour tide which had swept the party to power in 1945 was beginning to turn by the end of 1949, and Attlee dissolved parliament on 3 February 1950. The recent redistribution of seats gave Eden the choice of either standing for the new seat of Stratford and South Warwickshire with its rural and safe Conservative areas, or Warwick and Leamington with its predominantly industrial population. He loyally chose to stand by Warwick and Leamington. At the general election on 23 February he was returned with a majority of 8,814 votes, a decrease in his 1945 result. The Conservative party made a better showing. In an election which saw the highest turnout of voters since 1910, 315 Labour members were elected against the Conservatives' 298.

The second Attlee administration, with its slender majority, clung to power for another nineteen months. It was a period of significant developments in Europe and of crises abroad. Early in the year Eden had turned his attention to Egypt's interference with shipping in the Suez canal and criticized the government's decision to recognize communist China as 'fortunate neither in its timing nor in its method'. Then the movement towards European integration seemed suddenly to lunge forward. On 9 May the French foreign minister, Robert Schuman, launched his imaginative proposals to pool the coal and steel resources of France and Germany under a single authority, with provisions for wider participation. Eden had followed developments in this field with the closest interest but with a steadily diminishing enthusiasm. He was now more convinced of the difficulties than the advantages of close British links with Europe. Bevin's isolationist reaction to the Schuman plan provoked a Commons debate on 26 and 27 June. Only under extreme pressure from his shadow Cabinet colleagues did Eden actually criticize the government for having missed an opportunity which would have benefited the interests of both peace and full employment in Britain. Within a year this major step towards European integration had been achieved. The European Coal and Steel Community was established with a membership composed of France, Germany, Italy and the three Benelux countries.

This issue, however, had been dwarfed by the dramatic news on 25 June that North Korean forces had invaded South Korea. Eden once again condemned the Soviet Union for her disregard of the rule of law in her foreign dealings. He fully supported Attlee's promise of assistance in United Nations action in Korea, and by August British troops were in action.

Early in 1951 further articles by Eden appeared in the press, a habit he had adopted after going into opposition. It provided him both with a platform for his views and further financial remuneration. Later in January he visited the British Army of the Rhine, spending some time with his son Nicholas, who was stationed near Paderborn. Returning to London, Eden spoke during a House of Commons debate on the need for co-operation with Germany. He reiterated a view basic to his beliefs that peace could only be preserved by warning potential aggressors in advance of the consequences of their actions. In May the outspoken Iranian prime minister, Dr Muhammad Musaddiq, nationalized the Anglo-Iranian Oil Company with its vast refinery at Abadan, thereby terminating a concession renegotiated as long ago as 1933. Eden called for firm handling of the dispute. He was careful not to commit himself to a forceful solution. The Labour government preferred to await events. Attlee ruled out the use of force as both politically and morally wrong.

In July Eden visited Canada and the United States. His reception was warm, and he became a familiar face on North American television. He was back in London on 4 September and in the following month he presided at the twenty-first birthday celebrations of his son.

The Labour government, internally divided, weakened by the death in April of Ernest Bevin, damaged in popularity by the Iranian oil crisis and the austerities imposed by the Korean war, dissolved parliament on 5 October. The Conservative election manifesto contained a novel proposal for an excess profit levy, aimed at offsetting profiteering in the armament industries. It was known that this had particularly appealed to Eden, who in his campaign concentrated to an unusual degree on housing, agriculture and economic problems. On polling day, 25 October, Eden retained his seat with a slightly increased majority of 9,803 votes. The Conservatives regained office with a lead of twenty-six seats over the Labour party. It was an exhilarating moment for Winston Churchill, prime minister again. After a long uphill fight, and determined to avenge the defeat of 1945, he had led his party back to power.

When submitting his list of Cabinet appointments to King George VI, Churchill recommended Eden as foreign secretary and 'Deputy Prime Minister'. The king deleted the latter designation as infringing his constitutional prerogative to choose his prime ministers. The succession, however, was still understood to be Eden's. On 27 October he began his last spell as foreign secretary. He returned to the Cabinet with a refreshed mind and with all the authority of his past reputation as an expert diplomatic negotiator. So unchallenged was his position that at least one of his Cabinet colleagues, the home secretary, Sir David Maxwell-Fyfe (Lord Kilmuir), considered it a weakness of efficient Cabinet government, for he noticed that no other Cabinet minister felt competent to challenge Eden's authority. His position as foreign secretary was further strengthened by the fact that, unlike the wartime situation, Churchill was now to give him virtually a free hand both in the formulation and execution of policy.

The Churchill administration of 1951–5 was to prove one of the most successful peacetime governments since 1918. Part of that credit undoubtedly belongs to Eden. He was to work with increasing success at securing a *modus vivendi* with the communist world and establishing a satisfactory partnership with the European integration movement. Relations with the United States, however, were to pose continuing problems. Within the first month of taking office Eden outlined in speeches to the House of Commons and to a United Nations Assembly meeting in Paris the methods he intended to pursue in his foreign policy. He declared that the road to peace lay in 'preparation, conference and agreement: starting from small issues and working to the great'. This step-by-step approach was adopted by Eden for the solution of various difficulties affecting Europe, the Middle East and Asia.

The most immediate problem Eden faced was the need for a definite decision with regard to the latest step in the integration of Europe. In October 1950 the Pleven Plan had initiated negotiations on the formation of a European army in which national forces, including those of a re-armed Germany, would be fully integrated. Eden was pleased to see France and her traditional enemy, Germany, willing to co-operate on the formation of what became known as the European Defence Community (EDC), but he remained frankly hostile to the idea of Britain surrendering any of her sovereign rights or loosening commonwealth ties. He also had reservations about the practicality of the scheme, considering it too ambitious. He adopted the view, as had the previous Labour government, that while Britain could not participate in EDC, she would establish 'the closest possible association' with it. This was the position which Churchill and the Cabinet, despite some ministerial reservations, adopted. Eden therefore worked for a solution, with full support from the Truman administration, whereby Britain and the United States would, through their membership of NATO, 'help from without rather than participate from within'. Unfortunately the French government doubted British intentions and feared she would turn her back on the continent. It was largely through Eden's prodigious efforts that a satisfactory arrangement was achieved in the spring of 1952.

When Churchill and Eden visited Paris in mid-December they reiterated that Britain could only associate herself with EDC, but made a minor concession. They promised that British forces under NATO command would be linked with those of EDC. Further discussion of Britain's relationship with EDC took place in Washington where Eden accompanied Churchill in January 1952. The American secretary of state, Dean Acheson, came away with the impression that Churchill, while professing to take a helpful attitude towards EDC, did not in his heart approve of it. Eden explained his own position at Columbia University when he received an honorary degree. Referring to suggestions that Britain should join a federation of European states, he said: 'This is something which we know, in our bones, we cannot do.' British interests, he maintained, lay far from Europe. But continued support would be given to the cause of European unity.

After working out the form of Britain's association with EDC, Eden visited Paris on 1 February. He now found the astute and tenacious French foreign minister, Robert Schuman, dissatisfied. Schuman was anxious for a normal treaty relationship between Britain and EDC which would ensure mutual aid against aggression.

Only such an agreement would reassure French opinion, divided between treating Germany as a new ally or an old enemy.

The death of King George VI on 6 February brought to London many leading government officials, including Dean Acheson, Robert Schuman and Dr Konrad Adenauer, the German chancellor, pioneering his country's re-entry into Europe as an equal partner. Preparatory talks between these leaders enabled a communiqué to be issued on 19 February reaffirming Britain and America's agreement to maintain armed forces in Europe. At a NATO meeting in Lisbon later in the month conversations were continued over the future status of Germany and EDC. Throughout these meetings, and as late as 19 March when Eden was again in Paris, he fought stubbornly to resist mounting continental pressure for a firm treaty commitment instead of the projected offer of an Anglo–American guarantee to EDC. He even convinced the Committee of Ministers of the Council of Europe to form a closer association with the Defence Community. By the end of March, however, he had to tell the Cabinet that unless Britain was to be blamed for the breakdown of EDC a formal treaty would have to be concluded.

Agreement was finally reached by May and Eden flew to Bonn. On the 26th he signed on behalf of Britain the Bonn conventions, ending the Allied occupation and granting sovereignty to the German Federal Republic. The following day in Paris a series of agreements, linked to the Bonn conventions, were signed, thus establishing EDC. This was supplemented by a treaty of mutual security between Britain and EDC members, and by an Anglo–French–American declaration that any action threatening the Community would be regarded as a threat to their own security. In the cause of Allied unity Eden had committed Britain much further than he had himself originally envisaged. However, he had still preserved the principle that Britain would not delegate her sovereignty to any European supra-national organization. The long debate over ratification of EDC was to end only in August 1954 with its rejection by the French parliament.

Anglo–American relations were now being increasingly strained by events in Asia and the Middle East. Since assuming office Eden had been faced with growing evidence of Chinese communist support for the anti-French guerilla forces in Indo-China. Despite American assistance, fears began to grow that France was on the point of defeat and that communist China might intervene. Eden initially accepted the American view that France's struggle in Indo-China was in the general interest of containing communist aggression. On 26 May he discussed the situation in Paris with Dean Acheson and advised him about the limits of British support. Replying to Acheson's suggestions about a possible warning to China against interference, Eden stated that the British government would be opposed to any action likely to result in war with China. At another meeting later in June, this time in London, Eden managed to dissuade Acheson from issuing the warning. Meanwhile, Eden gave his full support to what seemed to emerge as France's overall strategy in Indo-China. This was to pursue the military battle until a position of sufficient strength had been achieved to enable a graceful withdrawal.

In the Korean war, as in Indo-China, Eden followed American policy so long as there was no danger of communist China being drawn into the conflict. His adoption of American thinking in that conflict, however, stemmed again from his experiences in the 1930s. Eden passionately believed that firmness paid. In the American response in Korea he was convinced the world was witnessing a display of the principle that the aggressor must never get away with it. But as with the Indo-China conflict, Eden's support had its limits. As the armistice talks between North and South Korea, begun in July 1951, progressed into the autumn, the American government began to fear that the North would take advantage of a negotiated respite and launch a major attack. Eden and Acheson discussed a suitable response to such a violation. It was agreed when Churchill and Eden were in Washington that Britain would join the United States in retaliation if the truce were broken. Eden held to the agreement reached by the previous Labour government that a Chinese attack across the Yalu river would be met with the bombing of communist airfields in Manchuria. After taking the advice of the chiefs of staff and discussing it with Churchill, Eden informed the State Department that Britain could not support a naval blockade of China.

The hazards British policy now faced as the subordinate partner in the Anglo–American relationship were vividly illustrated by the American bombing of power installations on the Yalu river, which were supplying the Manchurian airfields. The attack on 23 and 24 June was the closest to the Chinese border ever staged, and was undertaken without Britain being consulted. A storm of protest broke out in the House of Commons. Both Churchill and Eden defended the Americans, assuring the House that the action did not involve an extension of United Nations operations in Korea. To Acheson, who was in London at the time, Eden pleaded: 'No more surprises'.

If Britain followed the American lead in Asia, it was the reverse in the Middle East. Here relations with Egypt and the Sudan and the continuing dispute with Iran were the main British preoccupations. It was in this area of foreign policy that Eden hoped to make an impressive display of his talents and relevant experience. But it was the Middle East, that runs as a clear thread through his whole career, which was to shatter his reputation. The Labour government had sought a settlement of the oil dispute with Iran by taking the issue unsuccessfully to the International Court at the Hague and then to the United Nations. The United States, fearing a communist coup in Iran and the permanent loss of Iranian oil to the west, failed in its attempts at mediation. When in Washington in January 1952, Churchill, according to the memoirs of Dean Acheson, *Present at the Creation,* had criticized the Labour government 'who had scuttled and run from Abadan when a splutter of musketry would have ended the matter'. It was generally understood, however, that a forcible solution was out of the question.

Eden did not accept the American view that the only alternative to Musaddiq was communism. He was annoyed at the continued financial support given by Washington to the Iranian prime minister, who, in his view, had perpetrated a flagrant breach of contract. Strengthened in his assessment by powerful Treasury determination to protect British investments overseas, Eden adopted a firm stand, convinced that 'no agreement would be better than a bad one'. In February he persuaded the United States to cut off all military aid to Iran and reduce economic assistance to a trickle. Hopes for a settlement were suddenly raised in August. Internal political dissension in Teheran inspired a joint Anglo–American approach. Churchill was determined to give an elaborate American package deal a chance. This was rejected by Musaddiq, who now additionally demanded back taxes and royalties from the Anglo–Iranian Oil Company. By this point Eden was writing off the Iranian prime minister as a megalomaniac and a fractious child. Two months later Iran broke off diplomatic relations with Britain.

Churchill's intervention in the Iran oil dispute had been made possible because Eden was at the time on leave of absence. On 12 August news had been released that he was to marry Clarissa Churchill, the thirty-two-year-old niece of Winston Churchill. She was the daughter of Major John Spencer Churchill, a distinguished soldier, and Lady Gwendeline Spencer Churchill, daughter of the seventh Earl of Abingdon. Eden found in her a woman of wide cultural interests, with connections among the aristocracy and established literary world. The wedding took place at Caxton Hall on 14 August, with Winston Churchill as principal witness. Massive crowds waited outside to congratulate the newly-weds. After a reception at 10 Downing Street the Edens left for their honeymoon in Portugal. On his return to London at the end of the month Eden decided to sell his country home at Binderton, as he now had the use of his wife's cottage at Broad Chalke, near Salisbury.

The legacy of a colonial empire in the Middle East at a time of militant nationalism posed as many difficulties as it had once bestowed benefits. On 15 October 1951 the Egyptian government had unilaterally abrogated the 1936 Anglo–Egyptian treaty, which still had five years to run, and the 1899 Condominium establishing dual control over the Sudan. Anglo–American plans for a Middle East defence organization were also contemptuously rejected. This was followed by a demand for British evacuation of the canal zone and the Sudan. Eden replied that, while ready to revise the 1936 treaty, Britain intended to maintain her rights and allow the Sudanese to determine their own future. And in didactic tones he told the Egyptians that the unilateral denunciation of treaties undermined the entire structure of international relations. The issue of the Sudan was one where Eden's sense of principle was such that he would have resigned had he not got his way.

Anglo–Egyptian relations continued to deteriorate, culminating at the end of January 1952 in violent clashes and widespread arson in Cairo. Eden was prepared to commit British troops to quell the disturbances. Fortunately, order was soon restored. In the following months he continued to work on plans designed to give legitimate expression to Egyptian national aspirations while at the same time safeguarding Britain's position in the Middle East and the security of the canal zone. In doing so he had to resist growing pressure from the United States to surrender the Sudan and begin withdrawing British forces from Egypt. The State Department had embarked on a new policy of trying to ingratiate itself with revolutionary regimes in the Middle East. The deadlock, at least over Egypt's claim to the Sudan, was broken by a military coup on the night of 22–23 July. The corrupt King Farouk abdicated and was replaced by a junta of officers led by General Mohammed Neguib. He proved more amenable to negotiations. By the autumn he had dropped Egypt's claim to unity with the Sudan, which in November 1953 opted for independence. A review of British strategy which Eden had instituted late in 1952 resulted in a Cabinet decision to transfer the headquarters of the Middle East command to Cyprus. This opened up new possibilities for negotiations which he soon used to good advantage.

In September Eden briefly turned his attention to the competing claims of Italy and Yugoslavia to the territory of Trieste, where an Anglo–American force had been in partial occupation since 1945. On 18 September he flew to Belgrade to become the first foreign minister of a major western power to visit Marshal Tito since his break from the Soviet bloc. Trieste was discussed but no solution emerged until October 1954, when the disputed area was divided between Italy and Yugoslavia. Eden's visit was an imaginative stroke which resulted in Tito coming to London five months later.

Negotiations regarding an armistice in Korea had become bogged down over the question of the repatriation of prisoners, willing or otherwise. While supporting American insistence on the principle of no forcible repatriation, Eden actively involved himself in efforts to reach a compromise. In November he flew to the United Nations in New York to attend the meeting of the General Assembly. There he helped shape an Indian resolution on repatriation which the American government could accept. Dean Acheson, although he regarded these efforts as a 'cabal', and seemed annoyed by Eden's involvement, eventually agreed. On 3 December the Assembly endorsed the Indian resolution, advocating a repatriation commission. The skilful compromise was eventually accepted in June 1953. However, after the armistice was signed the following month, the State Department continued to harbour a sense of irritation at Britain's handling of the Korean issue.

The American presidential elections of November 1952 had brought victory to the war veteran and former NATO commander, Dwight D. Eisenhower, who appointed as his secretary of state

John Foster Dulles. Eden had always been able to establish the most intimate relations with previous American secretaries of state. It was to prove a great tragedy that he and Dulles were never able to work harmoniously together. Eisenhower revealed in his memoirs, *Mandate for Change*, that Eden had urged him privately not to appoint Dulles. A dedicated, knowledgeable man, particularly about the legal aspects of international affairs, he was what Eden termed 'a preacher in international affairs'. Eden was to find his sudden shifts of policy distressing and his tactic of 'brinkmanship' dangerous. Often Eden was unable to determine the precise significance to be attached to his words or actions. This resulted in growing tension and friction that clouded their judgment of personalities and events.

Early in March 1953 Eden, accompanied by the chancellor of the exchequer, R. A. Butler, visited Washington at the invitation of the president. Although economic affairs were the main topic of the nine-day visit, the new American administration was anxious to try and settle the Iranian oil dispute. Negotiations were now centred on Britain's demand for compensation for future oil profits. Eden was determined, as he wrote in *Full Circle*, 'to stand firm and not . . . allow ourselves to abandon points of principle in the face of blackmail'. For his part, Eisenhower was convinced that Musaddiq alone could prevent a communist coup. At last both he and Dulles bowed to Eden's preference against further compromise and for letting the deadlock continue.

Anglo–American agreement about Egyptian problems was not so easily reached. Heartened by Neguib's flexibility, Eden had been considering a settlement based on a phased withdrawal of British troops from Egypt, with the continued maintenance of a military base in the canal zone ready for use in case of war. This required the United States to be closely associated with some sort of Middle East defence organization and to provide assistance to Egypt. The bottom fell out of Eden's carefully laid plans when Neguib refused to allow American participation. He preferred to negotiate on evacuating British troops from Egypt. The wider problems of Middle East defence, he stated, would afterwards be considered.

Ill-health once again began to take its inevitable toll of Eden's physical and mental powers. In June 1952, after an attack of jaundice, he continued to suffer internal pains which were variously diagnosed and for which he had to give himself injections. In April

1953 X-ray examinations revealed the presence of gallstones. Churchill took over his duties at the Foreign Office, and on 12 April he was operated upon. Fever and jaundice led to another operation on the 29th, but his condition grew dangerously worse. An American specialist in Eden's particular condition recommended yet another operation. He spent a few weeks recovering his strength at Chequers and in early June was taken in a specially converted plane to the New England Baptist Hospital in Boston. An operation on his biliary tract was announced to have been successful. After a brief convalescence at the home of a friend in Newport, Rhode Island, followed by a stay on the French Riviera and a cruise in the Mediterranean, Eden returned on 5 October to the Foreign Office.

During his absence Eden had ironically come close to being appointed prime minister, for at the end of June Winston Churchill had suffered a stroke. Fearing the worst, he had written to Eden intimating that he might soon have to take over. But Churchill had remarkable recuperative abilities and an insatiable appetite for power. To have resigned at this point would have meant depriving Eden of his succession in favour of R. A. Butler.

The Conservative party conference in early October was able to welcome back Churchill and Eden, both restored to good health. Effective government now returned to Britain. In Eden's absence Churchill had been reluctant to make any major decisions, except in the area of relations with the Soviet Union. It was the only field of foreign affairs where Churchill felt his experience overrode the competence of his foreign secretary. In May Churchill had proposed a great power meeting, along wartime lines, to settle outstanding world problems. Contrary to the Foreign Office view, he believed that Stalin's death on 5 March had resulted in a new flexibility on the part of the Soviet regime. Continuous delays were to prevent the summoning of Churchill's obsessive project. Instead, Eden found that Adenauer and Georges Bidault, the new French foreign minister, had persuaded Dulles to explore the evident signs of a Soviet peace drive.

The ground for what was to become not a summit but a foreign ministers' conference was prepared in Bermuda. On 2 December Churchill and Eden arrived on the island for six days of conversation with Eisenhower and the French prime minister, Joseph Laniel. Churchill persuaded Eisenhower to agree to January talks in Berlin with the Soviets. Dulles, however, was to cause Eden a great deal of anxiety. He threatened that if the French government did not ratify EDC he would be forced into an 'agonizing reappraisal' of American policy towards Europe, hinting at a withdrawal of support for NATO and European integration plans. Dulles repeated this blunt warning when he again met Eden in London later in December. Unlike the French, Eden believed that Dulles was not bluffing.

The Berlin conference of British, French, American and Soviet foreign ministers was in session from 25 January until 19 February 1954. With regard to the future of Germany, Eden wished to propose a practical plan for reunification. This was to be based on free all-German elections for a representative government with whom a peace treaty would be negotiated. He knew that the Soviet foreign minister, Vyacheslav Molotov, could hardly agree to free elections, but considered that if the conference broke down at least Britain's position would have been made clear and the 'negative objective' secured, namely to encourage France to proceed with ratification of EDC.

The conference proved an almost total failure. Molotov rejected the 'Eden plan' for free elections, reunification and a peace treaty. He professed to believe that this was a device to compel Germany to adhere to western defensive organizations. For their part the western foreign ministers saw in Molotov's proposals a plan which would have indefinitely deprived the Germans of their freedom. And in Molotov's free use of the slogan 'Europe for the Europeans' Eden saw a device to undermine the whole system of western defence. The conference had also failed to make any progress on the long-standing problem of an Austrian peace treaty. Nevertheless, it had been useful as a continuation of the east–west dialogue and as a means of relaxing the tensions of the cold war.

At the Berlin conference agreement had been reached on a meeting in Geneva to discuss the questions of Korea and Indo-China. It was Eden who skilfully overcame Dulles' passionate objections to Chinese participation. After a long period of accepting the American contention that the French effort in Indo-China was a western interest, Eden began to draw back. The urgency of the meeting was further heightened in February and March as the French military position in Indo-China crumbled. Growing fear of possible American involvement in the fighting prompted Eden to canvass the view in Washington that partition with a western guarantee would be the least damaging of solutions. When the besieged French garrison at Dien Bien Phu seemed on the verge of surrender, the American government proposed to London and Paris that a joint warning be issued against Chinese intervention, backed by the threat of naval and air action against China and of intervention in Indo-China itself.

Eden did not intend to be 'hustled into injudicious military action' which he feared could easily lead to a world war. When Dulles came to London on 11 April he back-pedalled on a warning to China and talked instead of developing a South-East Asia defence organization. On both aspects of the problem Eden adopted a very cautious approach. To his great annoyance he soon discovered that Dulles intended to pursue the idea without consulting Britain about its future membership. Relations were further strained at the end of April when Dulles asked Eden, in Paris to attend a NATO Council meeting, to approve the relief of Dien Bien Phu by United States naval aircraft. 'I am fairly hardened to crises', Eden recalled in *Full Circle*, 'but I went to bed that night a troubled man.' He feared that the American plan would have been to get Britain involved 'in the wrong war against the wrong man in the wrong place'. He shortly discovered that Dulles was also prepared to move American armed forces into Indo-China, thereby internationalizing the French struggle.

Eden returned to London for consultations with Churchill and the Cabinet. He found complete opposition to any form of intervention. On 25 April the Cabinet refused to approve an American plan to send aircraft into action at Dien Bien Phu within three days. The French fortress fell on 7 May.

On 26 April the five-power conference had opened at Geneva. Having been the principal figure in deterring the United States from precipitate intervention in Indo-China, Eden threw his prestige into making a success of the conference, and he achieved this with skill and tenacity. He had already evolved a concept of the settlement that would be needed to bring peace to South-East Asia. He was determined to support a defence organization only to guarantee the results of the conference settlement. The initial prospects seemed dim. Dulles arrived at Geneva in a mood of apprehension and moral disapproval. He ignored the presence of the Chinese foreign minister, Chou En-Lai, and after a week returned to Washington. He was convinced that he could not get support for America's policy of trying to contain communism in South-East Asia. His absence did not, however, remove the threat of American intervention, which continued to haunt the proceedings.

Eden's task was facilitated by the conciliatory attitude of Molotov, with whom he shared the chairmanship of the conference. The first hurdle was surmounted by all sides agreeing in principle to an armistice. A protracted dispute ensued about the composition of the supervisory commission. A breakdown was narrowly avoided in June by unexpected Chinese concessions which additionally enabled armistice agreements to be arranged for Laos and Cambodia. And with the election in France of a new prime minister, Pierre Mendès-France, pledged to a quick settlement, prospects suddenly brightened.

After returning to London and reporting on 23 June to the House of Commons, Eden accompanied Churchill to Washington. The visit was timely in view of the widening estrangement in Anglo–American relations. Tension between Eden and Dulles was acute. Furthermore, Eden was discovering that his views on Indo-China and his proposals for a settlement had shocked the United States. His name there had become synonymous with appeasement, and he was being accused of responsibility for a sellout of the free world. The Anglo–American rift was also reflected in a growing divergence between Churchill and Eden. The prime minister was annoyed at what he regarded as his foreign secretary's short-sightedness in endangering allied co-operation, which was essential for world peace. On the other hand, the Geneva conference had contributed to Eden's growing critical attitude towards the State Department. But nothing of this was revealed in Washington. There Churchill spent most of his time trying to persuade Eisenhower to participate personally in a summit meeting on peaceful co-existence with the USSR.

The Washington meeting satisfied Churchill, who managed to remove Eisenhower's doubts about meeting the Soviets. Eden succeeded in getting Dulles to accept partition as unavoidable in Indo-China. New ideas about a guarantee of the settlement were discussed and agreement reached to set up a study group to prepare for the establishment of what eventually became the South-East Asia Treaty Organization (SEATO).

Eden returned to Geneva on 12 July for the last phase of the conference. In a series of hectic meetings there and in Paris he persuaded Dulles to allow American participation in the closing phase of the conference. He then threw himself into the tedious business of framing draft agreements to finalize the settlements. Success on all outstanding questions was achieved by 21 July. A ceasefire went in to effect throughout Indo-China. Vietnam was divided at approximately the seventeenth parallel, and provision was made for future elections. There was no agreement, however, on a multilateral guarantee. The United States did not endorse the settlement, but took note of the various agreements and declared that it would refrain from using force to disturb them. The unification of Korea, also on the agenda at Geneva, had not been achieved, although henceforth both sides refrained from interfering in each other's affairs.

Speaking to the final session of the conference Eden stated that, while everyone could not be satisfied, the conference had achieved two results. It had ended a war which had lasted for eight years. It had also, hopefully, reduced international tension at a point of instant danger to the world. He concluded that all now depended on the spirit in which the agreements were observed.

Eden's satisfaction at having reduced world tension was shortly enhanced by further agreements which made 1954 a notable year in his career. Within a fortnight of leaving Geneva he was able to announce the end of Britain's two festering problems in the Middle East. Progress towards settling the terms of British withdrawal from the canal zone in Egypt was impeded by the government's insistence on the right of re-entry in case of emergency. Eden was also hampered by a vocal minority in the Conservative party and even Churchill's opinion, always privately expressed, which resented what seemed like a 'policy of scuttle'. An American concession in June, undertaking to support the principle of freedom of navigation through the Suez canal, gave impetus to the negotiations. This was further speeded by the conclusion of the Defence Ministry in London that in the nuclear age the base was no longer vital. On 27 July an Anglo–Egyptian agreement was reached. It provided for the evacuation of the base within twenty months, its maintenance by British civilians for another seven years, and its reactivation in certain emergency circumstances. Significantly, the agreement upheld the Constantinople convention of October

1888 guaranteeing freedom of navigation through the canal. The settlement with Egypt was debated on 29 July in the House of Commons. Eden defended it with the telling argument: 'What we need is a working base, not a beleaguered garrison.'

Eden's policy of allowing the Anglo–Iranian oil dispute to simmer in a state of deadlock was soon vindicated. Musaddiq had been deposed in August 1953 by a coup d'état. By December Eden had succeeded in restoring diplomatic relations with Iran, thereby enabling conversations to proceed without intermediaries. After a further eight months of delicate negotiations a solution was announced on 5 August. An international oil consortium, in which the British company retained almost half the shares, was set up to produce and market Iranian oil. A fixed sum was agreed upon as compensation for the Anglo–Iranian Oil Company. Eden's waiting game had demonstrated the weaknesses of the State Department's tendency to be stampeded by fear of offending nationalism in the Middle East.

Much of Eden's remaining time as foreign secretary was concerned with negotiating pacts of regional defence against the threat of Soviet nuclear parity. The Geneva settlement had accelerated work on the American project for an anti-communist front in South-East Asia. On 8 September agreement was reached at the Manila conference to establish SEATO. However on 30 August the French Assembly, on a procedural question, had failed to ratify EDC. Eden was bitterly disappointed, but as he wrote in *Full Circle*, he saw no cause to put France 'like a naughty girl in the corner'. He moved quickly to save what he could of this basic building block in European integration.

Down in his Wiltshire cottage it occured to Eden that the problem of binding Germany into a system of western defence could be solved by admitting her into NATO and transforming the Brussels pact of 1948 into a mutual defence treaty. Additional advantages were that without the supra-national features of EDC Britain could be a full member, the movement towards a united Europe could be maintained, and domestic opposition to an increased British military contribution on the continent would be stifled. This was to prove Eden's finest hour.

Churchill and several principal Cabinet ministers agreed with this new approach. On 11 September Eden left for a diplomatic reconnaissance of the continent. He was greatly encouraged by the favourable response he found in Brussels and Rome. The German chancellor, Dr Konrad Adenauer, still a firm believer in the ideal of European unity and determined to restore full German sovereignty, agreed to membership of NATO. As a measure to re-assure France, he was prepared to accept self-imposed limitations on German rearmament. The prospect of British participation was additionally welcome.

On arriving in Paris on 15 September, the last and most sensitive capital of his tour, Eden heard the unpleasant news that Dulles had suddenly decided to pay a flying visit to Bonn. Eden regarded this as a dangerous intrusion into the pattern of unanimity he had already consolidated. Fortunately the intrusion proved irrelevant. It was through sheer perseverance at finding solutions to every objection raised by Mendès-France that Eden, after two days of intensive discussions, convinced him of the necessity for Germany's entry into NATO, with sufficient safeguards for France.

The attitude of the United States was the last remaining obstacle. Eden realized how great was the appeal of a united Europe to American opinion. During a brief meeting in London with Dulles, who was returning to Washington, Eden heard further threats of a possible withdrawal of American assistance to Europe. In reply Eden emphasized that his solution was the only im-mediately practical step towards real European integration. Dulles reluctantly accepted this appraisal.

A nine-power conference of Britain, France, Germany, Italy, the Benelux countries, the United States and Canada was convened in London on 28 September at foreign ministerial level. As a final concession to ensure French agreement, Eden had beforehand obtained Churchill's concurrence for 'some striking *quid pro quo*'. Acting in his capacity as chairman of the conference, Eden was able to choose the moment of his announcement. In a dramatic intervention on 30 September he announced that Britain would maintain on the continent its current four divisions and tactical air force, with guarantees against withdrawal. This unprecedented commitment was accepted by the French. It was to provide the permanent political basis of western defence. This commitment, Eden told the Conservative party conference on 6 October, was 'given to prevent a war and not win a war'. The decisions taken at the London conference were finalized in Paris on 23 October and came into force in May 1955. The agreement ended the occupation regime in Germany, admitted her to NATO and transformed the Brussels organization into Western European Union, henceforth a part of NATO defence.

Eden's historic achievement of ending European post-war antipathies and keeping the Americans committed to European defence deserved the compliments and praise which followed. Even Dulles could not help paying tribute to his 'resourcefulness'. The Carnegie Foundation awarded Eden the Wateler Peace Prize, and the *Daily Mirror* named him 'Politician of the Year'. Formal recognition of his success came when he was made a knight of the garter. The honour was conferred on 20 October by Queen Elizabeth. He now readily accepted the title Sir Anthony Eden, though both he and Winston Churchill had rejected knighthoods in July 1945.

The satisfaction of international achievement was only disturbed by the personal, and politically sensitive, problem of Churchill's retirement as prime minister. The position of 'crown prince' which Churchill had conferred in wartime was, as Eden remarked in *Full Circle*, 'not necessarily enviable in politics'. Unfortunately, Churchill's views on the subject of his retirement, as the diaries of his physician Lord Moran vividly illustrated, were prone to sudden changes, dependent on the prime minister's moods and health. Moreover, he felt passionately that his stature as the elder statesman could be useful in the field of international affairs. He continued, therefore, to fight the pressure to retire, determined that the decision would be his. During the summer he had had numerous conversations with Harold Macmillan, the housing minister. In his memoirs, *Tides of Fortune*, Macmillan revealed how he continuously and forcibly put to Churchill the case for retirement. He reminded Churchill that Eden had been led to believe on several occasions, and once categorically in a letter, that he would hand over by the latest in September. Macmillan was convinced that the continued uncertainty over the premiership was having disastrous effects. The government had ceased to function efficiently, Cabinets were long, wearisome and too frequent, ministerial changes were overdue, the parliamentary party was on the verge of breaking out into cabals, and the party machine was losing its grip.

On 18 October Churchill signified that he did not yet contemplate resignation. Cabinet changes were announced that day. Eden had all this time been immersed in foreign affairs. He had not taken part in the discussions leading up to the government re-organization. Nor for that matter had he allowed himself to be involved in any way in the preoccupation with Churchill's position. But his Cabinet colleagues noticed that the continued uncertainty had left him very nervy. Parliament was reconvened on 30 November to coincide with Churchill's eightieth birthday. That seemed to have been a watershed for the prime minister. By the end of the year he was proving more receptive to Macmillan's advice. This consisted of the argument that as 1955 was a suitable election year, that as the choice of the election date should rest with his successor, and that of the two possibilities, spring or autumn, the former was preferable, Eden should be given the succession early in the new year, form a new government and call an election.

As part of the process of arranging regional defence schemes, Eden now turned his attention to the Middle East. Despite previous failures a solution soon emerged. At the end of 1954 the Iraqi prime minister, Nuri es-Said, wishing to strengthen the 'northern tier' of Arab states, signed with Turkey on 24 February 1955 a pact of mutual co-operation known as the Baghdad pact. This strengthened the treaty negotiated a year before between Turkey and Pakistan. Eden regarded the arrangement as a potential 'NATO for the Middle East'. With Iraq already a British ally, the pact would help maintain British influence in the Middle East and act as a counterweight to Egypt. He readily obtained Cabinet approval to open negotiations for Britain's accession to the pact. Under State Department influence, Dulles drew back from associating the United States with the new regional arrangement. He aimed at blocking communist penetration, for which wider Arab participation was needed. And Egypt had already declared her opposition to the arrangement.

On 19 February Eden departed on a 15,000-mile tour of the Middle East and Asia, buoyed up by a closely guarded secret which Churchill had imparted to him. 'I have given Anthony a date when I shall go. I shall not go back on that now', Churchill told Lord Moran two days later. The date was 5 April and this time Churchill was to remain true to his word. In Cairo, on his outward journey, Eden had his first and only meeting with Colonel Gamal Abdel Nasser, who in November 1954 had replaced Neguib as president of the Revolutionary Council. Nasser declared that his basic sympathies were pro-western, but he refused to waver in his opposition to the Baghdad pact. 'No doubt jealousy plays a part in this and a frustrated desire to lead the Arab world', was how Eden reported to London his assessment of Nasser's attitude. The new Egyptian leader impressed Eden rather curiously as 'a fine man physically', and their talks on the whole were friendly.

In Bangkok from 23–25 February, Eden participated in organizing the permanent structure of SEATO. The occasion enabled him to discuss with Dulles a dangerous increase in tension between communist China and the United States. This had resulted from Chinese threats to seize the exposed islands of Quemoy and Matsu, held by Chiang Kai-shek's nationalist government in Formosa. At the end of January the United States committed itself to defend the islands and Formosa against attack. At the same time, in the House of Commons, Eden declared that he did not regard the two as in the same category, and on 4 February he expressed his fear about the dangers to world peace inherent in the dispute. In correspondence with Churchill, Eisenhower maintained that the nationalist Chinese, after the withdrawal of the French from Indo-China, had become the base for the western democracies' position in South-East Asia. There comes a point, Eisenhower wrote, where 'further retreat becomes worse than a Munich'. The offshore islands dispute, therefore, could not but bring out Anglo–American differences. Acting under Eisenhower's instructions, Dulles tried unsuccessfully to convince Eden of the importance of America's determination to stand by Chiang Kai-shek. It seemed to Eden that the risk American policy was running was disproportionate to the objective.

On his return trip Eden visited Delhi, where for the second time in his career he addressed the Indian parliament. In Baghdad he discussed with Nuri es-Said the progress in negotiations for Britain's accession to the Baghdad pact. Reporting to the House of Commons on 8 March after his return to London, he urged that the nationalist Chinese withdraw from Quemoy and Matsu in exchange for negotiations towards a final settlement. In *Mandate for Change*, Eisenhower described this suggestion as 'more wishful than realistic' and quite unacceptable. Fortunately, the expected showdown over the offshore islands never materialized.

In the House of Commons Eden had also been able to describe the progress being made towards the realization of a defensive agreement for the Middle East. Almost his last act as foreign secretary was to inform parliament on 30 March of the completion of these negotiations. Britain adhered to the Baghdad pact on 4 April. Pakistan joined in September and Iran in October. Eden could look back with satisfaction at the process he had nurtured since becoming foreign secretary, for security arrangements now covered the area from the Atlantic eastwards to the Pacific.

5

PRIME MINISTER
1955-1956

SIR ANTHONY EDEN, the 'crown prince', became prime minister
on 6 April 1955, at the age of fifty-seven. Perhaps the smoothest
changeover in British politics aroused little public excitement, not
least because the national newspapers were on strike. Eden himself
admitted in *Full Circle* that the long years of waiting helped to
dampen his exhilaration at attaining the premiership. On Tuesday
5 April, Winston Churchill took leave of his Cabinet colleagues
and tendered his resignation to Queen Elizabeth. On Wednesday
Eden followed to Buckingham Palace to kiss hands on his appointment. Churchill took a last affectionate look at the Cabinet room
at 10 Downing Street and departed for Chartwell, his country
home. That afternoon Eden faced the House of Commons for the
first time as prime minister to pay the traditional tribute to his
predecessor. In a lifetime of parliamentary speeches his effort on
this occasion was more of an ordeal than usual. His few words of
tribute to Churchill's political vision, magnanimity, humour and
command of the English language were received kindly by the
House.

To succeed Churchill meant inevitable comparisons. Eden did
not have the Churchillian rhetoric or personality. But he brought
to the premiership the legacy of having served under four prime
ministers, most notably Stanley Baldwin, from whom he drew his
main inspiration. Baldwin had groomed him and given him both
confidence and opportunity. It was from Baldwin that he was to

adopt the habit of frequent consultation alone with each of his principal Cabinet colleagues. This enabled Eden to support ministers authoritatively, and streamlined the work of Cabinet meetings. It was from Baldwin, too, that he adopted a vision of his premiership as one of uniting and serving all sections of the nation. Moreover, he had never forgotten Baldwin's dictum that a Conservative prime minister should be left of centre, enabling him thus to influence the floating vote to his left. Finally, Eden brought to the premiership an unprecedented wealth of experience in foreign and commonwealth affairs, and habits of diligence, thoroughness and application. He could count on an abundance of popular appeal and goodwill. His few detractors could only point to an undeserved reputation of inexperience in domestic and financial affairs. Few would have pointed out that his formative experiences were pre-war and might not be totally applicable to the changed power structures of the mid-1950s.

Eden acted quickly on two pressing questions. On 7 April he announced several Cabinet changes, leaving a major reshuffle for later. The first choice for his own vacancy in the Foreign Office was his close friend Lord Salisbury, a man of exceptional experience and qualifications. As Lord Cranbourne he had resigned with Eden in 1938, and during the war he had served as dominions secretary. When Eden was ill in 1953, Salisbury had successfully taken over the Foreign Office. But instead Eden appointed Harold Macmillan, who had been a marked success as housing minister since 1951, and briefly, though less happily under Churchill's shadow, as minister of defence. Undoubtedly, in the heady atmosphere of becoming prime minister, Eden's impulse was to divest himself of the Foreign Office with which he had so long been associated. Moreover, with the unhappy precedent of Neville Chamberlain in mind, he did not wish to repeat the procedure of having his foreign secretary in the Lords, and consequently have the additional work of that office burden him in the Commons. Macmillan had impressed Eden with his 'active and fertile mind'. Before the end of the year, however, Macmillan was to be replaced.

The Ministry of Defence now went to Selwyn Lloyd, who had previously had a long spell as minister of state for foreign affairs before becoming minister of supply. In that post he was succeeded by Reginald Maudling who had made his mark at the Treasury. Eden chose Gwilym Lloyd George, later Lord Tenby, the son of the former prime minister, to take over the Home Office from Vixcount Swinton. He and Lord De La Warr were the only two members of Churchill's Cabinet to be retired. A somewhat surprising appointment, in view of his previous experience as parliamentary private secretary to Neville Chamberlain, was the appointment of Lord Home (Sir Alec Douglas-Home) as commonwealth relations minister. Eden found his comparative youth an important recommendation. Including Edward Heath, who was then the deputy chief whip, the government now contained three future prime ministers.

By 15 April Eden had taken another major decision. After consulting his Cabinet colleagues, he announced in a television broadcast that a general election would take place on 26 May. He told the nation that 'uncertainty at home and abroad about the political future is bad for our influence in world affairs, bad for trade, and unsettling in many ways'. Constitutionally, Eden did not have to call an election until October 1956, but the Conservative majority was small, the economic situation was on the whole favourable, and public opinion seemed disposed towards the government. Eden was also inclined to seek a fresh mandate as a figure in his own right, rather than as Churchill's nominee for prime minister. Rather courageously he decided to take the risk of a general election, even though the results could snatch from him the fruits of long years of waiting. In anticipation of a forthcoming election, Clem Attlee had produced an exceedingly apt quotation in his welcoming comments to Eden on 6 April. When Lord Melbourne was hesitating to accept the premiership, Attlee stated, a secretary is alleged to have said: 'Why, damn it all, such a position was never held by any Greek or Roman, and if it only lasts three months it will be worth while to have been Prime Minister of England'. To which Eden replied that Melbourne had remained prime minister for a long time, in fact six years.

During the Easter parliamentary recess, R. A. Butler put the final touches to his budget. After a period of three and a half years of successfully restoring public finances, and producing a surplus of £282 million, he decided on a major concession. His budget in the House on 19 April lowered the standard rate of income tax from 9s to 8s 6d. In doing so Butler had ignored a February rise in the cost of imports and a drain on the country's gold and dollar reserves. But Eden considered that after certain precautionary measures then taken, Butler was fully justified in increasing public purchasing power. Immediately, and not unnaturally, charges of having produced an 'electioneering budget' were laid against the government, and were to become a prominent election issue.

The election of May 1955 was a quiet one. The Conservative slogan, 'Invest in Success', was difficult for the Labour party to fight. Eden's overall election strategy was to cut criticism of his opponents to a minimum. It was to appeal on his record in international affairs and a progressive social policy at home. His election address opening the campaign asked for a mandate to work for peace abroad and the creation of a 'property-owning democracy' at home. 'More hope, more choice, more freedom for all' was the exhortation. He made effective use of the now vital medium of television, for which he had a natural talent. He carried off on 21 May a masterly face-to-face television appearance, without a script. Deprecating what he called 'slanging matches', he spoke less as a party politician and more as a responsible statesman.

Lord Woolton, the party chairman, had organized the campaign to put Eden forward as 'the new "young" Prime Minister'. Dangerous triumphal tours of the country were avoided. Instead he visited the maximum number of constituencies, if only for a short time. He mixed easily with people, spoke in halls, at open-air meetings, and was unsparing in his efforts. Throughout he was ably assisted by Lady Eden, looking young and charming, and bolstering Woolton's conception of the campaign. The Eden marriage proved indeed to be a valuable electoral asset. Lady Eden had overcome her original political diffidence and soon proved to be quite at home on the platform. In their private life, too, she had originally been horrified to discover her husband's enormous workload and took measures to ensure that he had a scheduled pattern of leisure. This was reflected in a more relaxed manner adopted by Eden and which was noticed by colleagues and electorate alike.

The Woolton strategy proved remarkably successful. On polling day, 26 May, Eden retained his own seat with an increased majority of 13, 466. The Conservative party was returned to power with 345 members, a gain of forty-three seats. Conservatives polled 49.7 per cent of all votes cast, against Labour's 46.4 per cent. For the first time in ninety years a government had returned with an increased majority. It was a well-deserved victory and Eden could now look forward to a full term of office, gained on his own merits.

Election celebrations were cut short by growing industrial unrest. On 29 May the locomotive men went on strike. This was in addition to an inter-union dockworkers' strike which had been in progress since 23 May, and strikes by miners, lightermen and busmen. On 31 May a state of emergency was declared. The breakdown in transport and the stoppage at the docks were having a serious effect on the economy. On 5 June Eden broadcast a review of the situation to the nation. He pointed out the grave damage being done to Britain's export trade. The harassed and over-worked minister for labour, Sir Walter Monckton, virtually a prisoner in his St James's Square office, struggled to stem the tide of industrial discontent. On 14 June the railway strike was called off. The dispute was referred to arbitration and a compromise wage increase was accepted. The dock dispute, which was proving more damaging nationally, was settled on 4 July after the intervention of the Trades Union Council.

Deeply troubled by the industrial strife which greeted his first weeks as prime minister, Eden reacted with both short- and long-term measures. He set up a Ministerial Committee on Emergencies which handled the day-to-day problems created by the strikers. He was in constant consultation with both trade union leaders and employers. After the end of the railway strike he invited representatives of the Trades Union Council and the Federation of British Industries to Downing Street for talks, in an attempt to stop the sharp antagonism which he saw developing between employed and employers. He was to be no more successful in solving this growing problem than any of his Conservative successors as prime minister. But he had two great advantages: an open mind and a conciliatory nature. He shared, therefore, the distrust of both sides of industry towards suggestions for legislation to control the unions and their leaders. Instead, he worked with some success in reviving the pre-1951 remedy of what was called a 'period of reflection'. This involved a compulsory twenty-one-day cooling-off period between a decision to strike and its implementation. As a recommended but not a legal procedure, it found some favour with the trade unions.

It was foreign affairs, however, which were largely to dominate the life of the Eden government. Among the more important questions was Britain's future status with regard to the growing movement towards European economic integration. Eden's premiership coincided with some of the most significant developments in that movement. The six powers – France, Germany, Italy, Holland, Belgium and Luxembourg – met on 10 June 1955 at Messina in Sicily. Already integrated in the European Coal and Steel Community, to which Britain was by then associated, they now agreed to begin preliminary work on the eventual setting up of 'a common European market, free from all tariff barriers'. A Cabinet meeting at the time agreed to send a British representative, in response to an invitation, to participate in the work of the preparatory committee. Eden then found himself in sharp disagreement with Harold Macmillan, who as foreign secretary could at long last press from a position of power his convinced pro-Europeanism. Eden had genuine doubts about the common market plan in view of Britain's other obligations. Butler and many Treasury advisers shared these anxieties. Nevertheless, Macmillan pressed ahead, trying to devise an alternative plan in which Britain could take the lead. He fully realized that the weight of opinion, not only in the government, but in parliament and the press, was against joining the common market as a full partner. By the end of the year, he recalled in his memoirs *Riding the Storm*, the situation 'was one of doubt and uncertainty'.

Winston Churchill had retired with his dream of 'a top-level meeting without agenda' unrealized. Eden had always disliked the idea, feeling that such an unbusinesslike gathering, necessary in war, was unsuitable in peace. This was a view shared by Macmillan. He envisaged a four-power meeting as the beginning of a prolonged dialogue between east and west, proceeding over a period of time and continued later at foreign secretary level. This appealed to Eden, and during May and June Macmillan skilfully prepared the ground by personal visits both to France and the United States. On 26 May the Soviet government, now headed by the prime minister, Marshal Nikolai Bulganin, and with the party secretaryship in the hands of Nikita Khrushchev, accepted the joint western invitation to a summit conference at Geneva to open in July. The road to the conference had been considerably smoothed by a new gesture of reasonableness on the part of the Soviet leadership, who had agreed, finally, to the signature on 15 May of an Austrian peace treaty.

The Geneva conference had nominally been designed to identify problems and prepare the ground for future discussion. This was the only basis on which the United States was prepared to participate. Eden wanted it to achieve a definite, even if a limited, result. He believed that the western powers had a strong negotiating hand and should keep the initiative by having a previously prepared set of proposals. Another 'Eden plan' therefore emerged. It envisaged the demilitarization of a narrow strip of territory on both sides of the Iron Curtain, a limitation of armaments within specified areas of Europe, and a security pact. Macmillan was given the difficult task of selling these ideas abroad – a job he carried out with success and extreme efficiency, if not total enthusiasm. He was already making his mark as a very able and independent-minded foreign secretary.

Final preparations for the five-day Geneva conference were made at a meeting of foreign secretaries in Paris on 15 July. Eden and his wife arrived at Geneva on the 16th, staying at the same eighteenth-century house he had used during the Indo-China conference. During the course of the conference Eden elaborated the set of proposals he had formulated. He hoped thereby to place the Soviets in the position of finding them difficult to reject, and possibly making some progress towards the overall goal of German reunification. The Soviet contribution, introduced by Bulganin, ignored the 'Eden plan' and maintained that German reunification could only be achieved within the framework of a European security pact. Security and not German unity was his primary interest. From the round of opening statements Macmillan had managed to elicit four topics where common ground might be found: the reunification of Germany; European security; disarmament; and the development of contacts between east and west. These were the subjects which then occupied the conference. The result was a directive to the foreign ministers of the four powers to meet in Geneva in October for continued discussions.

Harold Macmillan, attending his first top-level meeting, was impressed by 'the great waste of time' involved. He was reminded by Eden, however, that important consequences flowed even from debates over the establishment of an agreed agenda. As an example of this dilemma, Eden recalled in *Full Circle*: 'which is the cart and which is the horse in European affairs. Does the union of Germany come first and bring security, or must security be established by some wide European pact before any kind of unity within Germany can be contemplated?' The conference failed to resolve this problem. Even the directive for the future foreign secretaries' conference, after much wrangling, had to merge these two items into one paragraph, thereby avoiding giving precedence to either.

Despite the almost total lack of agreement, the conference had been amicable and had contributed to the reduction of tension between east and west. It had also illustrated the point that peace was in fact being preserved and not endangered by the nuclear balance. Nuclear weapons were seen as having a deterrent power as formidable as their destructive capability. On his return to London Eden spoke of the conference as having successfully achieved agreement on the nature of outstanding problems, charted the course towards their solution, and reduced mistrust between east and west. Conscious perhaps that the pace of his first weeks in office had forced him to ignore Churchill, Eden invited the former prime minister to lunch at Downing Street. Churchill afterwards described Eden as not optimistic, but impressed by the friendliness of the Russians.

The conference had provided Eden with his first opportunity to meet the new Soviet leaders. Bulganin struck him less as a military figure than as a professional man who 'might be cast for the family doctor in a novel by Turgenev'. He was more impressed by Khrushchev, considering him vigorous, stubborn and with a sense of humour. In the course of a private meeting with the Soviet leaders, Eden politely turned down an invitation to visit Moscow. Instead, he extended to them an invitation, immediately accepted, to come to London. The visit was subsequently arranged to take place the following spring.

The problem of Cyprus now began increasingly to occupy Eden's attention. Since early in the year the British authorities on the island, acquired by Disraeli in 1878, had been faced with a mounting terrorist campaign. A small guerilla group, EOKA, was fighting for the union of the island with Greece. The Turkish government, feeling responsible for the Turkish-Cypriot minority in Cyprus, wished to see the status quo preserved. The withdrawal of the British garrison from Egypt meant that Cyprus had assumed a new importance in British strategic planning, and the reorganization of military bases on the island was being pressed ahead with. As both Greece and Turkey were members of NATO, Eden felt compelled to preserve peace between the two allied countries.

The continuing disturbances on the island forced the Cabinet in

June to proceed along the lines recommended by Macmillan and the colonial secretary, Alan Lennox-Boyd. This was to persuade the Cypriots to accept a liberal measure of self-government, even if self-determination was out of the question. As a first step, invitations were sent to the Greek and Turkish governments to participate in tripartite talks in London. On 30 June Eden described these developments in the House of Commons. The Turks responded favourably; the Greeks hesitated and then accepted. Chances for a settlement seemed very dim. Archbishop Makarios, the 'ethnarch', or Cypriot leader, considered the conference a 'trap' designed to delay bringing the Cyprus question to the United Nations and to impede the basic demand for self-determination.

The conference met in London on 29 August and broke down on 7 September. Eden had hoped the conference would, at the very least, convince hostile world opinion that 'old-fashioned British colonialism' was not the root of the problem. Rather, the irreconcilable demands of Turks and Greeks made a solution impossible: the former demanding, the latter refusing self-determination. The constitutional proposals which the British government had so carefully prepared were presented to both sides, more as a formality than with any hope of their acceptance. As the conference dispersed, bombings were renewed with increased ferocity on Cyprus, while anti-Greek riots broke out in Istanbul and Izmir. Additional British reinforcements were sent to the island, and on 15 September EOKA was banned. In addition, Eden replaced the governor of Cyprus with the retiring chief of the imperial general staff, Field-Marshal Sir John Harding. His blend of diplomatic and military qualities combined, for a time, to keep down the level of violence. Eden regarded the Cyprus problem as similar to that of Trieste, which he had successfully resolved by finally imposing a solution. He was determined to continue the search for a peaceful solution along these lines.

In the early summer the economy had begun to show dangerous signs of strain. Despite his natural absorption with foreign affairs, Eden took an active interest in economic matters and kept in close touch with the chancellor of the exchequer, R. A. Butler. Before departing for the Geneva conference, he gave Butler permission to introduce new financial measures designed to enforce a 'credit squeeze'. From June onwards the exchange value of sterling was below parity, gold and dollar reserves were falling, and the balance of payments was becoming unfavourable. It was clear that difficult times lay ahead. On 25 July Butler announced in the House of Commons a series of credit restrictions and cuts in expenditure by government authorities and nationalized industries. It was a difficult and unpopular decision to have taken so soon after the April tax cuts.

The economic situation continued to deteriorate during August and September. Butler realized that an autumn budget was necessary. On 30 August Eden ordered him to 'put the battle against inflation before anything else'. Such a step, Eden realized, meant further curbs on both government and private spending. He insisted that no cuts were to be made in Britain's atomic energy programme, but sanctioned a reduction of expenditure for nationalized industries, an increase in the rate of tax on distributed profits, cuts in housing subsidies and government building, new incentives for savings, and, what Eden seemed to have found most difficult of all, increasing by one-fifth the purchase tax on all goods, including for the first time pots and pans. In *Full Circle* he ruefully commented: 'It is difficult to advocate a property-owning democracy to the tune of "Your kettles will cost you more".'

Butler introduced his supplementary budget on 26 October. The inevitable criticisms were voiced that the full extent of the economic crisis had been hidden from the electorate in April. The opposition took the unusual step of tabling a censure motion accusing the government of incompetence in their economic policy. Eden himself wound up the debate by defending the April budget against charges of electioneering deception. The end of the budget debate did not put an end to the prime minister's anxieties about the economic situation. It was in particular the battle against inflation that absorbed him. His ideas on the subject, which he discussed with the chancellor of the exchequer and elaborated in a major speech at Bradford early in the new year, were not novel. But they had the benefit of being clear and defined. As he told his Bradford audience, Britain was suffering from 'the plagues of prosperity'. Economic expansion had inevitably brought with it demands for higher wages and rising prices. He therefore favoured a savings campaign to wipe up surplus spending, the continuation of the credit squeeze, and restraints in dividends and expenditure generally. He wished to see the creation of a sense of partnership in industry, and, more boldly, he called for the distribution of increased profits, in the form not of higher dividends but of lower prices.

Obvious domestic difficulties in the autumn were matched by more subtle problems abroad. The foreign ministers' conference which met at Geneva from 27 October to 16 November ended in deadlock. No progress was made on any of the directives prepared for it in July. The Soviet government was displaying a sudden rigidity in its approach to international relations which both puzzled and worried Eden. A more significant long-term development had already been foreshadowed on 27 September. Nasser announced that he had signed an agreement with Czechoslovakia for the supply of an impressive array of modern weapons. The Israeli government was naturally alarmed. British intelligence soon confirmed that the deal involved considerable quantities of MIG fighters, Ilyushin jet bombers, tanks and other heavy armaments. From the Soviet point of view it was a highly successful move into the Middle East and a useful counter to the recent Baghdad pact. Nasser declared that the arms purchases implied no pro-Soviet orientation in Egyptian policy. This was followed by a further announcement on 10 October that the Soviets were to assist in various Arab development projects, including the ambitious high dam at Aswan to harness the waters of the Nile.

Eden's initial reaction to the situation in the Middle East was to take what he called 'some positive action' in the hope of conciliating Nasser. If confidence and security could be restored to the Middle East, he told a Guildhall audience on 9 November, by Israel and her Arab neighbours reaching a frontier settlement, then the United States, Britain and possibly other powers would formally guarantee both sides of the dispute. Although twice questioned in the House of Commons on the implications of his remarks, Eden refused to elaborate. His hopes that this surprise proposal would encourage Arab–Israeli talks were quickly dashed.

For some time Eden had been contemplating a major reconstruction of the government. He had been sounding out colleagues since September with a view to shaping a Cabinet which would bear his distinctive imprint as prime minister, and which he finally announced on 20 December. R. A. Butler, chancellor of the exchequer for more than three years, who had recently suffered the loss of his wife, and whose last budget had received a very critical reception, was made lord privy seal and leader of the House.

Harold Macmillan was moved to the Treasury to provide a strong replacement for Butler. Eden had found it difficult to work with so forceful a personality as Macmillan, three years his senior. It was only with very great reluctance and on the condition that his position in the government would not be inferior to Butler's, that Macmillan acceded to the prime minister's wish. The Foreign Office was given to the congenial defence minister, Selwyn Lloyd, the only available minister with some relevant experience and one who could be relied upon to permit Eden to keep his hand firmly on foreign policy. Selwyn Lloyd was succeeded by Sir Walter Monckton, who was totally exhausted from the summer's labour problems and who could now relax in the less exacting position of the defence ministry.

Opportunity for advancement was given to younger ministers. Iain Macleod, formerly at the Ministry of Health, became minister of labour, and Robert Carr, who had served as Eden's parliamentary private secretary, was given a similar position with the Ministry of Labour. Enoch Powell, elected to parliament like Macleod and Carr in 1950, was given his first position as a junior minister with the Ministry of Housing. Finally, Edward Heath was further rewarded by promotion to government chief whip. These changes forced the retirement of such elder Conservative figures as Captain Harry Crookshank and Lord Woolton. The Cabinet was now a well balanced team with a stimulating infusion of younger talent.

Earlier in the month, on 7 December, Clem Attlee had announced his retirement after twenty years as Labour party leader. Eden had hoped that Herbert Morrison, whom he respected as 'a formidable and ingenious opponent', would succeed Attlee. Instead, Hugh Gaitskell, a younger, donnish figure was chosen. Eden was never able to establish with him anything like the close relations he had enjoyed with previous Labour leaders. It was to prove, as he later admitted, 'a national misfortune', particularly when a crisis situation demanded mutual confidence between government and opposition.

By the end of 1955 Eden's honeymoon period as prime minister came to an end. Vague mutterings and rumours of discontent with his premiership began to surface. Even *The Times* was becoming impatient with what it regarded as the delay in unfolding the character of Eden's government. On 3 January 1956 the traditionally pro-Conservative *Daily Telegraph* bitterly attacked Eden for alleged changes of mind, half measures and indecisiveness. Randolph Churchill, in a series of biting articles in the *Evening Standard*, made similar accusations. These criticisms soon gave rise to speculation that Eden intended to resign and make way for Butler.

'Anthony was very susceptible to such criticism', Lord Butler wrote in his memoirs, *The Art of the Possible*. And in his opinion Eden unwisely took an unprecedented step for a prime minister who had been in office for only ten months. He issued a statement from 10 Downing Street describing the reports as 'false and without any foundation whatever'. In his Bradford speech on 18 January Eden denigrated certain unnamed 'cantankerous newspapers' for publishing 'baseless reports of disunity'. Butler himself did not help the situation by hurriedly replying to a reporter's question that Eden was 'the best Prime Minister we have'. This remark immediately received wide publicity.

The dangers of the Middle East situation, the failure of the foreign ministers' conference, increasing anti-western pronouncements from Bulganin and Khrushchev, and a deteriorating situation in Cyprus, turned Eden's thoughts towards a Washington visit. He had for some time been intending to accept an honorary degree from Harvard University. Accompanied by the foreign secretary, Selwyn Lloyd, Eden sailed to New York, where he arrived on 30 January 1956 for his first American visit as prime minister. This was not a particularly auspicious time to be seeing Eisenhower. In September 1955 he had suffered a heart attack. It was only on 29 February 1956 that he was to announce his decision to run for another term of office. Throughout the four-day visit, therefore, the interest of Washington and Eisenhower himself was centred on the future elections.

The Washington talks, with no fixed agenda, ranged over a wide canvas of world affairs. China's admission into the UN, the Middle East and Egypt in particular, new schemes for economic integration in Europe, and the perennial German question were all discussed. Overall agreement on major issues outweighed several minor differences. On the important problem of Middle East security, Eden could not persuade Eisenhower to be more forthcoming towards the Baghdad pact. But on Egypt they agreed that Nasser should be treated as a friend until he proved otherwise. For the meantime it meant disregarding his vitriolic attacks against the Baghdad pact and the Jordanian regime. The official talks ended with Eisenhower and Eden issuing a joint 'Declaration of Washington', reaffirming Anglo–American unity of purpose in the defence of democracy.

The visit was capped by addresses Eden delivered to separate sessions of the Houses of Congress. He referred to recent Soviet probes into the Middle East which combined blandishment and threat. 'We do not intend to base our policies on the revival of old threats or the creation of new ones', he reassured the Senate. After fulfilling his engagement at Harvard and enjoying a brief but relaxing stay in Ottawa, Eden and Selwyn Lloyd arrived back in London on 9 February.

During Eden's absence abroad the new chancellor of the exchequer, Harold Macmillan, was grappling with increasing economic difficulties. Gold and dollar reserves were still falling, the credit squeeze, intensified by Butler's October budget, had not produced the desired effects, and the balance of payments was further deteriorating. Macmillan contemplated, but rejected, the drastic expedient of a sterling devaluation, or instituting a floating rate for the pound. Instead he embarked on the approach since known as 'stop-go', periods of economic expansion alternating with restrictions and restraints.

By the end of January Macmillan was convinced that more drastic action was needed. On his return from Washington Eden decided to sanction further restrictions on spending and cuts in expenditure. In deciding where these were to fall, he became involved in a threatening dispute with Macmillan. Eden's Cabinet had always worked well together as a team, and meetings were smooth, business-like affairs. But in *Riding the Storm* Macmillan revealed for the first time that a crisis as to where cuts in expenditure should fall threatened Cabinet unity. He had decided that the government should remove the existing subsidies on bread and milk. Eden was determined to oppose this, arguing that it would lead to an increase in the cost of living. On 11 February Macmillan wrote to the prime minister hinting that he would resign on the issue. Eden sent a delegation of three Cabinet ministers to see the chancellor. 'They said P.M. was absolutely determined not to give in on Bread and Milk', Macmillan wrote in his diary on 14 February. 'In that case, I replied, he must get another Chancellor.' The next day a compromise was worked out, reducing the subsidy on bread and delaying until July similar action on milk.

On 16 and 17 February Macmillan announced in the House of Commons a series of anti-inflationary measures supplementing the October budget. They included an increase in the bank rate, larger hire-purchase deposits, cuts in food subsidies and expenditure by the government, and the suspension of investment allowance for capital expenditure in industry. These measures were received critically but not unsympathetically by the Labour party. The situation, Macmillan realized, was still serious but not yet dangerous.

The Middle East was meanwhile perceptibly shaping up as the focus for a cold war power struggle. Nasser's vision of Egypt spearheading a revived Pan-Arabism, combined with the beginnings of an obvious Soviet revival of interest in the area, were being arrayed in a region of traditional British interest and against the new defensive perimeter of the Baghdad pact. The United States, condemning both communism and colonialism, remained an uncommitted bystander. It would have taken vision, foresight and the skill of a juggler to have avoided a clash where nationalism, frontier disputes and great power rivalry were so intertwined.

The focus of interest in March settled on the Hashemite kingdom of Jordan and its twenty-year-old ruler, King Hussein. The Jordanian government had become a battleground with interests competing as to its future alignment. Having lost its position in Egypt, the British government was now faced with an equally serious situation in Jordan. As a bribe to the young king to join the Baghdad pact, Eden had sanctioned the sale of Vampire fighter aircraft and a gift of free military equipment. This was not attractive enough to counter the sustained propaganda campaign being waged by Egypt against Jordan.

On 1 March King Hussein abruptly dismissed General John Bagot Glubb, the British chief of staff of the London-financed Arab Legion, one of the finest fighting forces in the Arab world. By acting against this near-legendary figure, Hussein hoped to strengthen his own authority, curb the rising tide of nationalism, and satisfy discontent among the Jordanian armed forces. With Selwyn Lloyd out of the country, it fell to Eden to deal with the emergency. Hussein at once assured him that the coup against Glubb did not affect his wish to continue cordial relations. Eden deeply resented this humiliating blow to Britain's prestige and military standing in the Middle East. But he reacted with commendable caution. He was determined to do nothing that would drive Hussein to further irrevocable extremes, and least of all to allow indignation at Glubb's dismissal to be a cause of a break in Anglo–Jordanian relations. Finally, he was anxious to continue the policy of trying to draw Iraq and Jordan closer together.

This approach of 'tolerant restraint', while a successful diplomatic response, proved disastrous for Eden's domestic reputation. The opposition demanded an immediate debate. Their criticism of British inaction was shared, too, by the small though vocal 'Suez group' of Conservative MPs. One of its members, Julian Amery, son-in-law of Harold Macmillan, wrote to *The Times* protesting against 'the bankruptcy of the policy of appeasement in the Middle East'.

On 7 March the House of Commons debated the Jordanian situation. By preference and habit Eden decided to make the winding-up speech. Hugh Gaitskell had already described the new dangers facing the Middle East. Conservative backbenchers had voiced their opinions including suggestions that Britain should intervene with military force. Eden later admitted that, from the parliamentary point of view, the speech was regarded as one of the worst in his career. He had basically told the House that he could divulge no details regarding the policy being adopted towards Jordan and the Middle East. It was an inconclusive speech which ignored the mood of the House and rebounded against him.

'I got well lectured in the House of Commons', Eden wrote in *Full Circle*. 'My friends were embarrassed and my critics exultant. There was a general comment that I had cut so poor a figure on a subject with which I must be familiar. But as diplomacy, the speech served its purpose.' It did indeed succeed in not exacerbating relations with Jordan, which eventually recovered. But Eden had been guilty of speaking to parliament as a foreign secretary and not a prime minister. What is more, he emerged from this episode with a personal and profound dislike for Nasser and his policy of Pan-Arabism, with its anti-western feelings and implicit military reliance on the Soviet Union. Despite assurances from Hussein and British observers on the spot, Eden could not help but suspect that Glubb's dismissal was Nasser's doing. According to Anthony Nutting, minister of state at the Foreign Office, Eden declared that he wished to see Nasser 'destroyed'.

Britain's position in the eastern Mediterranean was all this time being further threatened by the continuing problem of Cyprus. The strategic importance of the island was increasing as quickly as the Greek-Cypriots' demand for self-determination. In an effort to break the deadlock over negotiations Eden had approved in December 1955 a statement which was intended to reassure Makarios that the issue of self-determination could be discussed sometime in the future. This concession proved inadequate to satisfy the archbishop. Terrorism escalated on the island until on 6 March Eden approved the deportation of Makarios to the Seychelles islands. This display of toughness heartened the more extreme members of the Conservative party and helped Eden recover some ground lost by his parliamentary performance over the Glubb dismissal. But Eden's short term as prime minister prevented him seeing the resolution of the Cyprus crisis. It ended in 1959 with the establishment of a republic of Cyprus within the commonwealth. Its first president was Archbishop Makarios.

The rescue measures which Macmillan had announced in parliament in mid-February seemed to steady the economic situation. At the end of March the government published its White Paper, *The Economic Implications of Full Employment*. It had originally been planned by Eden as long ago as the summer of 1955, and was to have dealt with the causes of unrest in industry. As the year drew to an end, labour relations became a less pressing issue. Consequently, the White Paper as published dealt with action against inflation, calling for restraint in wage claims and fixed profit margins. Eden had the impression that the document was well received by the press. Macmillan, who had himself merely presided over its publication, thought the press received it with some derision.

Macmillan's own time was being taken up with the preparation of what turned out to be his first and only budget. He was in constant consultation with Eden during this time and formed the impression that the prime minister, like many highly-strung men, was more agitated by small worries than serious difficulties. At moments of real crisis Macmillan found him 'constant and determined'. And despite their earlier disputes over food subsidies, Macmillan generously wrote in *Riding the Storm* that Eden's 'judgment on domestic issues was always wise and based on imaginative understanding of the needs and ambitions of the mass of the people'.

In considering his budget proposals, Macmillan contemplated and then rejected an increase of 6d on income tax. Such a measure, undoing the concession of Butler's alleged electioneering budget, would have been disastrous for the former chancellor's reputation. Partly on political grounds, therefore, Macmillan opted for other measures. His budget, delivered on 17 April, continued the attack on inflation he launched in February. It was a 'savings' budget which, although including an unpopular increase in tobacco tax, seemed for the meantime capable of steadying the situation. Its main innovation included the premium bond scheme offering tax-free prizes, which reflected Eden's long-standing concern with savings. During the next two months Macmillan moved ahead, and succeeded in further reducing government expenditure, particularly defence costs. By July he could inform parliament that gold and dollar reserves had risen, exports were up and retail prices were steady. Extreme inflation was in fact beginning to be reduced.

Attention was distracted from the budget by the arrival in London on 18 April of Marshal Nikolai Bulganin and Nikita Khrushchev. The visit was in response to the invitation Eden had issued the previous year at Geneva. Despite the hard line the Soviet leaders had adopted in their recent pronouncements about the west and Britain's colonial legacy in Asia, Eden had decided that the visit should continue. He believed that the contact would be in the interest of peaceful relations with the Soviet Union, a policy he had set as the centre of his premiership. 'B and K', as the Soviet leaders were internationally known, were given a regal welcome from the moment their modern battle cruiser the *Ordzhonikidze* docked at Stokes Bay near Portsmouth harbour. Their itinerary included a sightseeing tour of London, dinner at 10 Downing Street, where the guests included Winston Churchill, an overnight stay at Chequers, a visit to Oxford, tea with Queen Elizabeth at Windsor, a reception at the Painted Hall in Greenwich, and a flying visit to Scotland. Interspersed between these formal engagements were talks that Eden regarded as the longest discussions on foreign relations in which he had ever participated. Khrushchev, for his part, later recalled that he had never before had such intensive contact with foreigners.

In a series of thorough-going talks at Chequers and Downing

Street, the subjects of Germany, disarmament and peaceful co-existence were fully examined. But this did not add anything to what had already been gone over in Geneva. Turning to the Far East both sides noted with satisfaction the reduction of tension in the offshore islands dispute between Formosa and China. It was on the Middle East that the toughest language was used. Eden told the Russians that the uninterrupted supply of oil was vital to the British economy. 'I said I thought I must be absolutely blunt about the oil, because we would fight for it', Eden recalled in *Full Circle*. It was his impression that this direct warning was understood by the Russians. Khrushchev's reaction, even as recorded by Eden, reveals that the Soviet leader was not impressed by threats. In a final gesture of goodwill, Eden accepted an invitation to make a return visit to the USSR.

Eden breathed a sigh of relief as the train carrying the Soviet leaders back to their cruisers pulled out of Victoria Station. The visit had been a complex undertaking and a calculated risk. A mammoth security operation had gone off well. Only two episodes had marred the occasion. A Labour party reception witnessed scenes of acrimonious exchanges with Khrushchev and Bulganin which had made press headlines. Much more serious was the affair of the frogman, Commander Lionel 'Buster' Crabb. On 19 April he had disappeared without trace while making an underwater inspection of the hull and propellers of the Soviet cruiser berthed in Stokes Bay. Crabb had been seen diving near the cruiser by the Russians, and early in May the Soviet government formally protested. Eden replied by acknowledging that the inspection had taken place, but stated that it had been done without permission, and offered his apologies. Questioned in the House of Commons, he took the unusual step of refusing to accept ministerial responsibility. It was done, he told the Commons, 'without the authority or the knowledge of Her Majesty's Ministers. Appropriate disciplinary steps are being taken.' The Soviets accepted Eden's explanation and his apologies. He told the House that he would not let the episode detract from the usefulness of the visit towards improved Anglo–Soviet relations.

In fact Eden took far more than just disciplinary steps. He made use of the tactlessness and incompetence the episode revealed to modernize the organization of the Secret Intelligence Service (SIS). The head of SIS was then Major-General Sir John Sinclair, known as 'Sinbad' because of his service in the navy, and his scheduled retirement possibly saved him from being sacked. The Portsmouth operation had in fact only been approved by junior members of SIS. Eden shook the complacency of the organization by selecting Dick White, the first-ever civilian, and, to add insult to injury, the current chief of the rival MI5 intelligence agency, to head SIS. The thoroughgoing reform which accompanied this change in leadership was a major achievement of Eden's premiership.

The Crabb affair did not deflect Eden from assessing the results of the visit and planning future strategy. He had assumed that peaceful co-existence with the Russians related to their tactics and not the long-term strategy. The nuclear stalemate had only forced them to revert to more insidious methods. It was not invasion which was the threat any longer, he concluded, but rather the dangers of Soviet infiltration. He immediately directed the Foreign Office to begin an intensive examination on how to meet this new challenge, with the emphasis more on economic and propaganda weapons than on military strength.

This re-examination was closely related to Eden's basic conviction that underlying many of Britain's economic problems were her over-extended defence commitments. By the mid-1950s Britain had world-wide defence obligations to the various regional security arrangements and her still considerable overseas territories. Soon after becoming prime minister, therefore, Eden had ordered drastic cuts in defence expenditure. He directed that these cuts should be aimed at the forces being maintained for the least likely risk, major global warfare. Despite the difficulties of reconciling the Treasury's demands for savings with the services' estimates of what was essential, substantial economies were made. Some overseas bases were scaled down, plans for the active and reserve fleets of the Royal Navy were reduced, and the programme for guided missiles was made less ambitious. In early July Eden held a series of discussions with relevant ministers on Britain's long-term defence needs, which, among other conclusions, led to a major reappraisal of NATO's strategy. It was now assumed that the advent of nuclear weapons made it possible to reduce conventional forces in Europe. Eden accompanied all these economies and changes with some important administrative reforms in the defence establishment. A permanent chairman was appointed to liaise between the chiefs of staff and the Ministry of Defence. At the same time it was contemplated that the powers of this ministry would be strengthened, but Eden was by then no longer prime minister.

The only part of Britain's defence to escape economies was the hydrogen bomb programme. On 7 June Eden announced in the House of Commons that the first hydrogen bomb tests would take place early in 1957. In reply to criticism, he later told the House that he was prepared to discuss with other governments the limiting and regulating of such explosions. A plan for international control and the limitation of tests was completed by December, but rejected at the Anglo–American Bermuda conference in March 1957.

From 28 June to 6 July Eden was host to an unusually difficult commonwealth prime ministers' conference. There was considerable discussion about Britain's forthcoming debut as a nuclear power, its implications for commonwealth relations, and possible peaceful uses for atomic energy. Equally contentious was the discussion about Britain's European policy. As chancellor of the exchequer, Macmillan had continued his efforts to produce an alternative to the projected common market which would be acceptable in London. By the end of May, however, the foreign ministers of the six had approved the report of the preparatory committee of the Messina powers. Plans then proceeded to draft an agreement on the common market, or European Economic Community, and a separate one on atomic co-operation. An interdepartmental committee, with which Eden kept closely in touch, could reach no agreement on British policy. With nothing definite having been decided, the commonwealth prime ministers could only issue general warnings against any form of British association with the common market. Eden was particularly sensitive to such criticism. Macmillan found the discussions ill-informed and excessively prejudiced.

In the following weeks Macmillan came down in favour of an acceptable compromise called 'Plan G', one of nine alternative schemes devised. This envisaged the formation of a European free trade area to which countries outside the Messina group of six would belong, and which would be associated with the commno market. Such a scheme would enable Britain to retain her advantageous commonwealth links without being bound by the rules of the Messina idea of a customs union. Macmillan apparently received strong Cabinet support from younger ministers, although the more senior members were hostile. Eden was finally convinced of the feasibility of 'Plan G' and allowed Macmillan to begin publicizing it. In October the Cabinet was to give its, in some cases, reluctant approval to this historic innovation. But by that time Eden was preoccupied with a serious Middle Eastern crisis in which the country had been gripped since July.

6

SUEZ
1956-1957

'THE lessons of the 'thirties and their application to the 'fifties are the themes of my memoirs', Sir Anthony Eden wrote in the foreword to *Full Circle*. One of the most important lessons he professed to have learned from his pre-war experiences was that a militant dictator's capacity for aggrandizement was limited only by the physical checks imposed upon him. For that reason Eden had praised America's decision to fight for the independence of South Korea, and had himself taken a firm line during the Anglo–Iranian oil dispute. It was not a lesson he believed need be applied to the Indo-China war or the Formosa straits crisis. But in Eden's view the Egypt of Nasser provided another test case for the application of the lessons of the thirties. The Suez crisis which began in July 1956 was to dominate Eden's premiership until his resignation on 9 January 1957. It has since become an event as controversial and synonymous with him as Munich had become with Neville Chamberlain.

The proposal for the high dam on the upper Nile at Aswan, which would have provided irrigation control and hydro-electric power, was regarded as the most ambitious attempt ever undertaken to solve Egypt's pressing economic and social problems. A financial loan for the project had been under discussion since late in 1955 between Egypt, Britain, the United States and the World Bank. In January 1956 Nasser had begun to balk at some of the conditions of the loan. He feared that the required guarantees would infringe upon Egyptian sovereignty. In the following months the dismissal of General Glubb, continuing anti-British propaganda emanating from Egypt, rumours that the Soviet Union had offered to finance the dam, growing anxiety at Nasser's Soviet arms deals, and increasing doubt about his ability to repay the huge loans under discussion, led Britain and the United States to reconsider their financial support for the dam. The two countries had arrived independently, but simultaneously, at this decision. By mid-July, according to Eden, the government had concluded that it could not support the project, which was likely to become an increasing financial burden on a strained economy. Eden would have preferred 'to play this along' and avoid the dangers of a precipitate announcement of withdrawal. But on 19 July, for a combination of domestic reasons, Dulles informed the Egyptian ambassador in Washington, Ahmed Hussein, that the United States was withdrawing its offer of a loan. The decision was publicly announced the same day. Eden had been informed, though not consulted, about the American decision. His hand had now been forced by Dulles' historic miscalculation. On 21 July Eden made public a similar British decision. The World Bank loan, contingent on the Anglo–American grant, was thus cancelled. This brief sequence of events sparked off the Suez crisis.

Nasser reacted angrily in a speech on 26 July at Alexandria. He announced the nationalization of the Universal Company of the Suez Maritime Canal and the termination of its concession to operate the canal. Shareholders in the company, the majority of which were British, were promised compensation at current prices. In addition, Nasser implied that canal dues would be used to finance the Aswan dam. He raised thereby immediate fears about the proper maintenance of the vital waterway. Three-quarters of canal shipping belonged to NATO countries, while half of Britain's annual oil imports were transported through Suez. In one stroke Nasser had struck a blow at Britain's position in the Middle East, challenged the entire western world, and again reaffirmed his leadership of anti-colonialism in the Arab world.

Eden was dining at 10 Downing Street with his protégés and allies, King Feisal of Iraq and his foreign minister Nuri es-Said, when a secretary brought in the news of Nasser's speech. In Eden's mind everything now depended upon what he called 'the resolution with which the act of defiance was met'. He began to set the guidelines for action in talks that night with Cabinet ministers, the chiefs of staff, and French and American diplomats. The following morning he made a brief statement to the House of Commons. He promised that consultations would take place on the effect nationalization would have on the operation of the canal, as well as the wider issues involved. Hugh Gaitskell, the Labour party leader, condemned Nasser's 'high-handed and totally unjustifiable step'. Parliament was firmly united behind the government, and the press was almost unanimous in its condemnation of Nasser.

Under Eden's guidance the crisis was not allowed to centre on the legality of the act of nationalization, on which opinion was divided, or the financial arguments about Egypt's capacity to pay compensation and at the same time proceed with the Aswan dam. By the Constantinople convention of October 1888 Egypt was obliged to keep the canal open to all shipping. An even older agreement put the running of the canal in the hands of the Suez Canal Company. Its capital, directors, shareholders and employees were almost entirely non-Egyptian. From the beginning, therefore, Eden intended to site the dispute within its broader aspects as a flagrant breach of an international agreement. In *Full Circle* he described the scenario for the crisis thus: 'Theft would not have paid off, a breach of agreement would not have been endured, a wholesome lesson would have been taught in respect for the sanctity of agreements.' However consistent these principles may have been with his life-long political outlook, Eden was to pay a fatal price in trying to enforce them.

After the situation was fully examined on 27 July in the Cabinet and in consultation with the chiefs of staff, several critical decisions were reached which guided the actions of the British government throughout the crisis. Foremost was the decision that Nasser could not be allowed to control the canal in defiance of international agreements. The Cabinet agreed secondly that British interests in the Middle East had to be safeguarded, if necessary by military action, and in the last resort by unilateral force. The chiefs of staff were instructed, as Eden revealed in *Full Circle*, 'to get ready a plan and a time-table for an operation designed to occupy and secure the canal, should other methods fail. We hoped to count upon the participation of the French in any expedition which was mounted. We expected that the United States would at least be neutral.'

Immediate practical steps were then decided upon. Consultations were to begin with Paris and Washington to align a joint policy. No attempt was to be made to bring the issue before the Security Council of the United Nations, where the Soviet veto would block effective action. Economic and political pressures alone were to be initially directed against Egypt. Her sterling balances in London were blocked, the assets of the Suez Canal Company safeguarded, and a ban placed on further export of arms. At the same time a small ministerial Committee, the 'Suez Committee', was formed to keep in contact with the situation on behalf of the Cabinet. Its members included, besides the prime minister, Selwyn Lloyd, Macmillan, Lennox-Boyd, Lord Salisbury, Lord Kilmuir, and Peter Thorneycroft, the president of the Board of Trade. Butler, who was ill at the time, sometimes attended subsequent meetings of this inner Cabinet.

President Eisenhower was informed on the evening of the 27th of the momentous decisions taken that day in London. 'If we take a firm stand over this now we shall have the support of all the maritime powers', Eden wrote to him. 'If we do not, our influence and yours throughout the Middle East will, we are convinced, be finally destroyed.' Eden recommended a meeting at ministerial level between France, the United States and Britain. With John Foster Dulles away on a visit to Peru, Eisenhower sent Robert Murphy, deputy under-secretary of state for political affairs, to London with instructions to dampen down the crisis, discourage the use of force, and get agreement on a pacific course of action. Eisenhower was alarmed at the extreme reactions evident in London. He basically doubted the validity of the legal position being adduced as justification for using force and felt a negotiated settlement was feasible. In the following weeks he exchanged many telegrams and had numerous telephone conversations with Eden. The president frequently expressed the opinion, as he wrote in his memoirs *Waging Peace*, that 'the case as it stood did not warrant resort to force'. But his consistency in expressing this view tactlessly left the question open as to whether he would, as happened, condemn and resist the British use of force as a last resort. At this early point in the crisis Eden assumed that American policy reflected prudence rather than divergence. He made the mistake, however, of ignoring the forthcoming presidential elections of 6 November as a determining factor in Eisenhower's attitude.

Discussions between Selwyn Lloyd, Robert Murphy and Christian Pineau, the French foreign minister who had come to London, produced agreement to summon a conference of maritime powers. Although Murphy felt he had succeeded in momentarily defusing the situation, he had the impression that the British government had taken a firm decision to 'break Nasser' and initiate hostilities at an early date. In actual fact, Eden and the Cabinet knew by this time that there was no such possibility. Under the Anglo–Egyptian agreement of July 1954, the last British troops had been withdrawn from the canal zone on 13 June. The resources simply did not exist for a quick Anglo–French airborne assault on Suez supported by ground troops. Cyprus did not yet have the necessary facilities. Combined operations would have to be mounted from Malta, six days' sailing to Egypt. Within a few days the chiefs of staff were definitely to report that without American assistance it would take six weeks to assemble a joint Anglo–French force capable of re-internationalizing the canal.

On 30 July Eden informed the House of Commons of the measures so far taken by the government. He reaffirmed his intention not to allow the canal to be left under the control of a single power which could exploit it for national purposes. On 1 August Dulles arrived in London to participate in the tripartite foreign secretaries' talks. He carried a letter from Eisenhower which did not in fact rule out the eventual use of force. But the president emphatically restated American objections to this and stressed the political obstacles to the use of American military power overseas. This was, too, the line that Dulles took in his numerous conversations with British officials. The Americans hoped that prolonged negotiations would vitiate the desire for military action.

Eden participated in the foreign secretaries' meetings, and found himself in instant agreement with Pineau. The French were anxious to make a major contribution to a combined Anglo–French military operation. They had no allies to protect or large-scale defence interests in the Middle East, but they were fighting a nationalist rebellion in Algeria and believed that it was being aided and abetted by Nasser. Relations between Eden and Dulles, in contrast, had never been good, and the crisis was to cause a further deterioration. Eden adopted a strictly principled position, while

Dulles emerged as the improvizing diplomat, trying to find common grounds for agreement. Such an out-of-character role led the United States secretary of state into paths of tortured ambiguity. While denying that there was a legal case against Nasser, at the same time Dulles remarked that a way had to be found 'to make Nasser disgorge' the canal. This phrase particularly appealed to Eden, although it was an overstatement of American determination and led to a tragic misunderstanding between London and Washington.

A statement issued at the end of the talks reaffirmed the principle of international control of the canal and invited twenty-four nations concerned with its use to confer in London on 16 August. A Cabinet meeting on 2 August approved the policy so far adopted in the crisis. A negotiated settlement would be genuinely pursued and thoroughly explored. In the event of its failure, Britain would in the last resort use force. In his own mind Eden was determined not to let the negotiations drag on from conference to conference.

On 2 August parliament began a two-day debate on Egyptian events. Eden informed the House that steps were being taken to evolve an international authority which would ensure freedom of transit through the canal. The opposition was still largely in agreement with the government. Referring to the threats from Nasser's expansionist ambitions, Gaitskell stated that these were exactly the same as Britain had encountered from Mussolini and Hitler before the war. But Gaitskell added that so far Nasser had not done anything which legally justified military intervention and that force should only be used in accordance with the United Nations charter. For the meantime Eden seemed to be in control of the situation and leading a united government and country through a difficult situation.

In the fortnight preceding the opening of the London maritime conference, military and diplomatic preparations went ahead. The Mediterranean fleets of Britain and France began to assemble. Bomber squadrons flew from their British bases to Malta. Army reservists were called up and merchant shipping and civil aircraft were requisitioned by the government for troop movement. On 7 August infantry and artillery units were flown to Malta and Cyprus. Three days later an Anglo–French military committee began meetings in London to plan the invasion. The most important diplomatic activity now centred on the Soviet Union. Eden was satisfied that Bulganin and Khrushchev had recognized Britain's special interest in the Middle East. The prime minister attributed this to the warning he had given in London to the Soviet leaders on the vital importance of Middle East oil to the British economy.

Gaitskell had not in fact been the first to equate Nasser with the dictators of the thirties. At the end of July the press had immediately conjured up analogies with Hitler and Mussolini. A Labour MP had spoken similarly in the Commons on 28 July. The consensus began to emerge of the nationalization gesture as equivalent to Hitler's reoccupation of the Rhineland in March 1936. Just as that was the alleged moment to have stopped a programme of German expansion, so, it was now argued, the time had come to curtail Nasser's expansionist ambitions. Eden agreed to the extent, as he wrote in *Full Circle*, that it was 'important to reduce the stature of the megalomaniacal dictator at an early stage'. He also admitted to seeing various similarities, mainly in the use of propaganda, between Nasser and Hitler and Mussolini.

It was not until his nationwide broadcast on 8 August that Eden used the current analogy. He developed his ideas about an international system for the canal and assured his audience that he did not seek a solution by force. But an act of 'snatch and grab' could not be allowed to succeed. Britain had had previous experiences of unilateral denunciations of international treaties. That was how 'fascist governments' behaved, he said, and concluded: 'Our quarrel is not with Egypt, still less with the Arab world; it is with Colonel Nasser. With dictators you always have to pay a higher price later on.' This was the first public indication that Eden's target was not just the canal, but Nasser himself.

The first cracks began now to appear in the bi-partisan approach Eden had secured in the House of Commons. Gaitskell warned the prime minister, both in writing and at 10 Downing Street, that the opposition would not back the use of force unless deployed through the United Nations. Eden could offer no satisfaction on this point, and felt that Gaitskell had ratted on his original position. Labour support for the government henceforth melted away. In retaliation Eden was to conceal government plans from the opposition until the eve of military operations. It was a major disaster which ended with a divided country going to war.

The first London conference, attended by twenty-two of the twenty-four nations invited, opened on 16 August. Egypt refused to participate on the grounds of the implied threats against her, while Greece made the Cyprus situation the excuse for her absence. Eden opened the proceedings with a warning that all participants had a common interest in preserving the sanctity of international agreements. Dulles then elaborated a mainly American-inspired plan, which was discussed and accepted on 22 August, but only by eighteen states. The plan took the form of a declaration which recognized the sovereign rights of Egypt, promised fair compensation for the use of the canal, reaffirmed the principle of international control, and proposed the setting up of a board, including Egypt, which would run the canal on a non-political basis. Although Eden failed to convince Dulles personally to visit Nasser to present the eighteen-nation proposals, he felt satisfied with the results of the conference, for the United States had presented and was associated with the projected solution.

The Australian prime minister, Robert Menzies, who was at the time in London, set off to Cairo at the head of a five-man delegation to seek the agreement of the Egyptian government. He was the most fervent commonwealth supporter of the British position in the crisis and, as an old acquaintance of the prime minister, had been relied upon for advice and encouragement. Menzies arrived on 2 September in Cairo, where he and his committee spent six days in friendly but fruitless talks. Going beyond his brief, Menzies warned Nasser that Anglo–French military preparations were not a bluff. Nasser was unimpressed, for at a press conference on 31 August Eisenhower had committed himself to a peaceful settlement of the dispute and nothing else. The Menzies mission ended in failure with Nasser having decided to reject the eighteen-nation proposal and just sit tight.

The momentum of negotiations appeared to have halted. Eden had meanwhile been considering the consequences of the anticipated failure in Cairo. The crucial decision was again taken not in London, but Washington. In an exchange of five letters from the end of August to 8 September, Eisenhower tried to leave Eden in no doubt about America's attitude to the use of force. In reply to his exhortation to continue showing a firm front in the crisis, Eden received on 3 September what he called a 'disquieting' response. Eisenhower wished to see the issue of the canal, on the one hand, and policy towards Nasser's position in the Middle East firmly separated. The president wrote that American public opinion flatly rejected the use of force, and it was doubtful whether Congress would support even limited American military intervention.

Replying on 6 September, Eden reaffirmed his intention to continue negotiations, and concentrated on trying to convince Eisenhower that the Suez canal and Nasser's ambitions were not separable. The latter were equated in detail with the tactics of Hitler's policy of foreign aggrandizement. Eden argued that the world had witnessed the 'opening gambit' in Nasser's strategy to expel all western influence from the Middle East, possibly deny oil to western Europe, and grant an open door to the Russians. Although conscious of the dangers of military intervention, Eden wrote, 'it would be an ignoble end to our long history if we accepted to perish by degrees.'

On 8 September Eisenhower again tried to moderate Eden's more extreme interpretation of the crisis, accusing him of inflating the importance of Nasser. The president expressed his misgivings about preparations for the Anglo–French military expedition. He conceded that eventually there might be no escape from the use of force. But to do so while avenues for negotiation still remained would produce the most serious consequences.

This correspondence left Eden with little room for manoeuvre. He was not yet prepared to defy his American ally. But the European canal pilots were ordered to leave their posts in the hope that the disruption of ship traffic could create the pretext for intervention. And in concert with the French government, Eden decided to overcome his previous reluctance and appeal to the Security Council. He drafted a resolution condemning Nasser and appealing to him to reopen negotiations on the basis of the London conference proposals. Dulles immediately declined to be associated with the move. He suspected that it was not an honest attempt to reach a solution, but a cover for action against Egypt. Furthermore, he had in early September evolved yet another plan to head off any movement towards military operations. His ingenious scheme, which became known as the Suez Canal Users' Association (SCUA), envisaged the users of the canal clubbing together to run and manage passage of their shipping. A share of the tolls, paid direct to SCUA, would be passed on to Egypt. The weakness of the plan was that it ultimately depended on coercion if Nasser refused to co-operate. No attempt was made at this stage to clarify the anomaly.

The SCUA plan was given detailed consideration during the visit to London on 10 September of the French socialist prime minister, Guy Mollet, accompanied by Pineau. It had been six weeks since Nasser's coup and the occasion proved a timely meeting of heads of state. Pineau especially disliked the idea of SCUA and regarded it as another Dulles bluff. Eden argued that it was the least objectionable of a limited number of undesirable options. After further discussion it was agreed that the plan should be supported. It was a critical decision which aroused misgivings in London. It involved deferring reference of the dispute to the United Nations. It also meant delaying the departure date for the military expedition (operation 'Musketeer'), now fully prepared, from 15 September to 1 October.

Harold Macmillan, a leading Hawk, was particularly disillusioned with Dulles' latest scheme, but acquiesced under the impact of the financial dimension of the crisis. Foremost was the need to keep in line with the American government. A military operation posed certain threats to the position of sterling which only Washington could remedy. Selwyn Lloyd, uncomplainingly sharing his duties with the prime minister, preferred an immediate recourse to the United Nations. But the Cabinet endorsed Eden's approach on 11 September and thus embarked on the ultimately futile SCUA road.

Parliament, recalled from its summer recess, debated the situation on 12 September. The cost of keeping in step with the United States was disunity in the House of Commons. The tone of the debate and the comments offered were extreme on all sides. Eden, opening for the government, revealed details of SCUA, and implied that if necessary it would be backed by force. The opposition pressed the government to ignore the latest American plan and go immediately to the United Nations. This is precisely what Eden would have preferred had he not bowed to American pressure.

On the second day of the debate the government's policies were torpedoed by Dulles. At a press conference he had underminded the mutually agreed SCUA plan by declaring that he never envisaged force as a part of it. The United States did not intend to shoot its way through the canal. Whatever misunderstanding there might have been during the framing of SCUA, such a blunt statement destroyed the ambiguity regarding the use of force which had appealed to Eden when first presented with the plan. This latest Dulles performance irrevocably shattered the final vestige of Anglo–American trust.

The immediate consequence of Dulles' remarks was to give Eden one of the stormiest and most humiliating days he had ever experienced in the House of Commons. He had to continue supporting an emasculated proposal for which he remained solely responsible against an evident display of Anglo–American disunity. Furthermore he now faced mounting pressure, even within the Conservative party and from such Cabinet ministers as R. A. Butler, to give a pledge not to use force except after reference to the Security Council. Eden successfully resisted this pressure, telling the House that such a pledge could not be given in advance. He weakened his case, however, by then assuring members that if circumstances allowed the dispute would be referred to the Security Council. That evening the government won a vote of confidence in its handling of the situation.

Eden was furious with Dulles, and henceforth the two men were scarcely on speaking terms. The prime minister now came to the conclusion that in future he would take the initiative and no longer follow the American lead. An indication of his determination not to be deflected was his reply to an unexpected letter from Bulganin criticizing Anglo–French military preparations and warning that 'small wars can turn into big wars'. Eden replied on 17 September, ignoring the threat and emphasizing Anglo-French efforts to produce a peaceful settlement.

The second London conference opened on 19 September with the eighteen states previously in agreement attending to discuss SCUA. Nasser had already declared his total opposition to the idea and announced that he would resist its implementation with force. By this time, too, Egyptian pilots were successfully operating the canal, further reducing the ostensible justification for foreign management. The conference completed its deliberations by 21 September. Only fifteen of the participating states agreed to join SCUA, which was to hold two meetings in October. The final blow to Eden's interest in the project was the agreement among members making payment to the association rather than to Egypt entirely voluntary.

Almost two months after Nasser's coup there was still no sustained pressure being exerted against Egypt. Reports reaching the Foreign Office suggested that the abysmal failure of the second London conference had encouraged a widespread belief, especially in Cairo, that the crisis was over. Equally disturbing to Eden were reports from the chief whip, Edward Heath, that there was trouble in the party. A growing number of Conservative MPs were opposed to the use of force even as a last resort. Meanwhile there had also been a substantial loss of gold and dollar reserves. Macmillan warned the prime minister that prolongation of the situation would result in Britain having to ask the United States for financial assistance.

It was precisely to bring the dispute to a head, therefore, that on 22 September Eden and Mollet decided that they would put their case to the Security Council, a meeting of which was later fixed for 5 October. This action was significantly taken without consulting Dulles. He was informed and angrily expressed his disapproval of the timing. On 26 September Eden and Selwyn Lloyd flew to Paris, actually in fulfilment of a long-standing engagement to discuss the common market. The French were eager for early military action. Eden reassured them that Britain, too, was prepared to use force to maintain the international status of the canal. It was agreed that the dispute would not be allowed to fester in a backwater at the United Nations.

On 25 September Macmillan, who was visiting Washington to attend a meeting of the International Monetary Fund, confided to Eisenhower that Britain's financial situation made it impossible to prolong the crisis without eventually asking for assistance. His most significant conversation was with Dulles, who explained that he had been hurt by the decision to take the dispute to the United Nations without his being consulted. There would be nothing but trouble in New York, he warned. In a press conference on 2 October he brutally disassociated the Eisenhower administration from the policies of the 'colonial powers' and said of SCUA: 'There is talk about the "teeth" being pulled out of it. There were never "teeth" in it, if that means the use of force.' This statement stung Eden, and was for him the final let-down. Anglo–American relations had reached breaking point.

Eden had been carrying a crippling burden of decision-making and negotiation in a major international crisis. Macmillan, who perhaps was in closer contact with the prime minister than any other Cabinet minister, wrote in his memoirs, *Riding the Storm*, of how impressed he was by the quiet confidence of Eden, who was facing the crisis with both physical and moral courage. On 5 October however the continued strain of events affected Eden's health. He had called in at University College Hospital to visit Lady Eden when he suffered a sudden high fever. Rather ignominiously, he was confined to the adjacent room where his temperature rose to 106 degrees. He spent the weekend at the hospital and recovered sufficiently to return to work. His sudden collapse was an indication of the recurrence of his previous bile duct trouble which was soon to undermine his health.

The proceedings at the United Nations, which opened on 5 October, lasted for eight days. Eisenhower was intensely suspicious that the Anglo–French move presaged the impending use of force. The Soviet government, which had on 28 September again warned Eden about a military move, adopted a belligerent attitude. The debates at the United Nations and the behind-the-scenes discussions ended in an impasse. They confirmed the Anglo–French standpoint, but brought a solution no nearer. The first part of the joint Anglo–French resolution suggested 'six principles' that should govern a Suez settlement. They included respect for Egyptian sovereignty, free and open passage through the canal, its insulation from the politics of one country, and provision for arbitration in disputes. This was carried unanimously by the Security Council. The second part of the resolution linked these principles with the proposals of the first London conference and SCUA scheme and invited the Egyptian government to negotiate on this basis. This was the part of the resolution which mattered to Britain and France. It was vetoed by the Soviet Union. Agreement on principles but without action had shadowed all of Eden's efforts since July. It was a situation he could no longer accept. The path of negotiation was ended.

The Conservative party conference was meeting at Llandudno during the closing stages of the Security Council deliberations. It was an occasion when the party closed ranks in enthusiastic support of the government. Anthony Nutting, minister of state at the Foreign Office, and within a month to resign in protest against government policy, delivered a stirring speech. He declared that Britain and France meant business and would stand firm. If the United Nations did not do its duty, Britain must do hers. Butler directed his attack against Dulles' views on alleged British colonial-

ism and appealed to the conference not to 'knuckle under to pre-
datory nationalism'. On 13 October Eden addressed the final rally
of the conference in an extremely robust and successful speech.
His remarks included the warning that 'with us force is the last
resort, but it cannot be excluded.'

A new dimension to the use of force now entered into the crisis.
Eden had originally decided that he wanted to keep the future
status of the canal separate from the knot of Arab–Israeli relations.
In order to get action he had preferred to keep the issues 'crisp'.
His personal sympathies were pro-Arab, although he resented
Egypt's refusal, in defiance of a United Nations resolution, to
allow Israeli shipping to use the Suez canal. Besides, Britain was
too treaty-bound to risk active intervention in the festering Arab–
Israeli dispute. These obligations arose from the Anglo–Jordanian
defence treaty of 1948, the Baghdad pact, and the tripartite
declaration of 1950 binding Britain, France and the United
States to prevent any violation of the Arab–Israeli armistice
lines.

The French government however had no inhibitions about
collaborating with Israel. It had been in close touch with Tel Aviv
since the early days of the crisis. Representatives from the respec-
tive Ministries of Defence exchanged information and then began
to co-ordinate military plans for joint intervention in Egypt. Only
hints of this collaboration may have been known to the British
government. By September Israel was receiving vast supplies of
French armaments. On the 21st the Israeli government decided
on a preventive strike against Egypt if Anglo–French plans could
be sufficiently co-ordinated.

Much of what flowed from this collaboration remains unclear.
Nor can one be precise until the official records for this period
become available, if even then, about the exact point at which
Eden and then the Cabinet discussed and agreed to what has
become known as 'collusion'; that is, a concerted, highly secret
plan – in this case for co-ordinated Anglo–French–Israeli military
action against Egypt – with the intention of denying the existence
of such collaboration. But on 14 October the French government
attempted to combine Israeli plans to attack Egypt with operation
'Musketeer'.

In order to encourage Israel to advance across the Sinai desert,
it was imperative to have the use of the only effective bomber

force available, which was British. Consequently two French emissaries, Albert Gazier, minister of labour and acting foreign minister in Pineau's absence abroad, and General Maurice Challe, deputy chief of staff of the French air force, were received by Eden at Chequers. According to Anthony Nutting, who witnessed the ensuing conversation, Challe outlined a plan to bring the canal under Anglo–French control. It broadly corresponded to subsequent events. Israel was to be invited to attack Egypt across the Sinai peninsula. Having given the Israeli forces time to occupy most of it, Britain and France would then order both sides to withdraw from the Suez canal. Intervention would follow on the pretext of separating the two combatants. If this was accompanied by the seizure of the terminal ports of the canal, Britain and France would control the passage of shipping and incidentally break the Egyptian blockade of Israel. Neither the timing of the operation nor military plans were discussed. Eden is alleged to have replied that he would consider the proposals and convey his response to Mollet. The whole scheme grated on Eden's natural reluctance to enter into any agreement with Israel.

The fact that the Middle East situation was beginning to look threatening was the only hint that Eden gave for visiting Paris on 16 October, accompanied by Selwyn Lloyd. The conversations with Mollet and Pineau took place in conditions of exceptional secrecy at the Hôtel Matignon. No other officials were present for most of the talks. Views were exchanged on the situation after the Security Council proceedings and on the development of SCUA. Then they considered what Eden described in *Full Circle* as 'the growing menace of hostility by Egypt against Israel'. He had in mind the tension between the two countries arising from Egyptian support for the fedayeen commando raids from Gaza into Israel; the long-standing blockade of Israeli shipping in the gulf of Akaba; and reports of a joint Egyptian–Syrian–Jordanian command, which was in fact established within a week. The Israeli government appeared to be poised for a preventive strike against one of its Arab neighbours. A French-supported Israeli attack against Jordan, allied to Britain, would have been a tragic nightmare. Eden took advantage of the Paris meeting to argue that 'if there were to be a break-out it was better from our point of view that it should be against Egypt. On the other hand, if the break-out were against Egypt, then there would be other worries, for example the safety of the canal. We discussed these matters in all their political and military aspects.' Here, clearly stated, is the trend of thought that convinced Eden in principle of the benefits of collusion.

There remained the question of Cabinet approval. In *The Art of the Possible* Butler described how on 18 October Eden summoned him into the Cabinet room at 10 Downing Street. The prime minister stated that it was suggested in Paris that in the event of war between Israel and Egypt 'we should go in with the French to separate the combatants and occupy the canal.' Butler was impressed by the audacity of the plan, which he agreed to support. His only reservation, brushed aside by Eden, was concern about the reaction of public opinion. Eden then reported on his Paris discussions to the Cabinet, emphasizing the growing danger that Israel would make some military move. According to his account, the Cabinet took no definite decision.

Eden's Cabinet had approved without dissent the decision of 2 August regarding the ultimate use of force to internationalize the canal. Each subsequent twist and turn of the crisis had inevitably produced shades of opinion. Some ministers were more in favour of Eden's anti-dictator line against Nasser, while others were mainly concerned with the future of the canal. Points of view ranged from that of Macmillan, who was prepared to pawn the pictures in the National Gallery to go through with the venture, to the more cautious approach of Sir Walter Monckton and the younger Iain Macleod. The crisis had placed additional burdens on the Ministry of Defence, which had been given to the ailing Monckton at a time when it was a relatively untaxing position. It was purely on the grounds of his ill-health that he had asked on 24 September to be relieved of his job. He formally resigned on 18 October and accepted the previously vacant office of paymaster-general with a seat in the Cabinet. Anthony Head, an ex-professional soldier, with personal knowledge of Nasser, and a close friend of Eden, was moved from the War Office to the Defence Ministry.

A curtain of secrecy now descended as Anglo–French policy went underground. British ambassadors abroad, allied military representatives in London, and the press were suddenly cut off from relevant information. The previous British ambassador in Washington, Sir Roger Makins, had left on 11 October. His replacement, Sir Harold Caccia, did not arrive until 8 November. On

19 October the Anglo–French invasion commanders were told to prepare to launch operation 'Musketeer', previously deferred, within ten days. The British government, however, refused to sanction any military move which could give the least suspicion of collusion with Israel. This fiction of non-collaboration was to be maintained for years to come. On 22 October the Israeli prime minister, David Ben-Gurion, informed the French government of his doubts regarding British resolution. Before committing the Israeli armies to a thrust across the Sinai desert he wanted cast-iron guarantees about the vital role of the British bombers in destroying the Egyptian air force. It has been alleged, therefore, that Ben-Gurion insisted on a written document, signed by the three countries concerned, finalizing all the arrangements. It is further alleged that during 23 and 24 October such a document was signed in a villa at the Paris suburb of Sèvres by Mollet and Ben-Gurion. Patrick Dean, deputy under-secretary of state at the Foreign Office, signed on behalf of the British government. The Israelis were now prepared to go into action against Egypt on 29 October.

The day of decision for the British Cabinet was 25 October. It was decided that, in case of a conflict between Egypt and Israel, Britain and France would at once call on both parties to stop hostilities and withdraw to a distance from either bank of the canal. Failure by either side to comply within a given time would result in Anglo–French intervention 'as a temporary measure to separate the combatants'. This action, it was considered, would safeguard the canal and arrest the potential spread of fighting in the Middle East. It had been a most difficult decision for Eden. He was conscious of the many dangers, not least that of complete inactivity in face of a widespread Middle East conflict.

Eden's determination to fight in the guise of a peacemaker meant that he could not permit the invasion fleet at Malta to begin combat-loading until after the expiry of the ultimatum. This condemned the operation to a possible ten-day delay, covering loading and sailing time to Egypt. Under French military pressure, however, the British commanders relented. On 27 October Anglo–French aircraft carriers sailed east from Malta. The next day the slower transport ships set off for their objective, Port Said. British Canberra bombers, flying at very high altitudes, kept watch on the canal and Egyptian troop movements.

On the morning of 30 October the Cabinet discussed the news that Israeli troops had crossed the Egyptian frontier and were striking across the Sinai peninsula. The situation considered five days before had now arisen. There only remained the matter of settling the terms of the ultimatum, which, it was decided, would be finalized with Mollet and Pineau on their arrival shortly in London. The Cabinet then approved the terms of a letter to Eisenhower asking him to support the action taken to safeguard the canal and stop the fighting. This message crossed with another from the president, who demanded to know what was happening between the United States and its European allies. He was outraged at having been kept in the dark and ultimately duped.

Complete agreement on all points of action and timing was reached over lunch with Mollet and Pineau. By 4.15 p.m. ultimatums had been presented to the Israeli chargé d'affaires and the Egyptian ambassador ordering the combatants to withdraw ten miles from the canal and setting a twelve-hour time limit for compliance. Eden, Butler and Selwyn Lloyd saw Hugh Gaitskell at about the same time and told him about the ultimatums. Gaitskell was furious at not having been previously consulted. The United States ambassador, Winthrop Aldrich, was likewise informed, as was parliament at 4.30 p.m. Eden conceded in retrospect that it was an error not to have given the opposition leader and the United States and commonwealth heads of government some prior notice of his intentions to issue the ultimatum. However, he believed that once 'palavers' began effective action would have become impossible.

Reaction to the Anglo–French action could hardly fail to be hostile. Eisenhower immediately warned Eden and Mollet of the consequences. Canada led the more outspoken commonwealth members in strongly expressing her disapproval. At the United Nations the Afro–Asian block was furious. In the Security Council, which had been convened at America's request, Britain and France used their veto powers for the first time. They rejected a United States resolution calling for the withdrawal of Israeli troops and for all countries to refrain from the use of force.

The ultimatum to Egypt and Israel expired at 4.30 a.m. on 31 October. The Israelis had accepted; they were still at least 100 miles east of the canal. The Egyptians naturally refused. After a Cabinet meeting that day the air offensive against Egyptian airfields began at nightfall. Nasser at once ordered blockships to be sunk in the canal. The invasion armada of warships, freighters and landing craft meanwhile moved towards the eastern Mediterranean. The very rigid planning had them scheduled to reach Port Said not before 6 November.

The air offensive against Egypt added fuel to the debate in New York and London. At the United Nations the dramatic rift in the Anglo–American alliance was clearly revealed to the world. Britain and France again had to use their veto in the Security Council. The House of Commons, sitting in almost continuous session, witnessed scenes of bitter controversy, frequent uproar, and on 1 November a rare suspension of proceedings. Eden concentrated on defending Israeli military action, explaining Britain's use of the veto at the United Nations, and emphasizing that Anglo–French military action was only a temporary move. The description he used was a 'police action'. In reply to the widespread comment in the House on the rift in Anglo–American relations, Eden bravely stated that Britain had to act to protect her vital interests in some circumstances without American agreement. The limits of this contention were one of the few lessons to be learnt in the following five days.

On 1 November Eden referred to an idea which was to provide a way out from the Anglo–French operation. He stated in the House that after the Egyptian and Israeli armies had been separated the United Nations might then wish to step in and physically take over the task of maintaining peace. This idea possibly originated in the Foreign Office. It was to be taken up and skilfully developed by Lester Pearson, the Canadian foreign minister. In the early hours of 2 November the General Assembly concluded a debate in an emotional and punitive atmosphere. Dulles had introduced a resolution calling for an immediate ceasefire. It was adopted by a vote of sixty-four to five with six abstentions. This was Dulles' last appearance in the Suez crisis. The following day he was rushed to hospital for an emergency operation for cancer.

On 3 November the British Cabinet decided to accept a ceasefire if a United Nations peace-keeping force was established, accepted by both Israel and Egypt, and maintained until a final settlement was reached. At this point it was hoped that limited detachments of Anglo–French troops would also be stationed between the combatants. Pearson proposed the establishment of such a UN force to secure and supervise the cessation of hostilities. The General Assembly passed the resolution without opposition, though with nineteen abstentions.

Military operations meanwhile continued in Egypt. By 5 November Israeli armed forces had unexpectedly attained their objectives. A two-pronged attack across northern Sinai had placed them just east of the Suez canal opposite Ismailia. A separate attack southwards had led to the capture of Sharm el-Sheikh, lifting the blockade of Israeli shipping at the mouth of the gulf of Akaba. In deference to British pressure Ben-Gurion agreed temporarily to postpone acceptance of the United Nations call for a ceasefire. Egypt had already notified its compliance.

At dawn on 5 November, a day prior to schedule, British and French paratroops were dropped over Port Said. The first of more than a hundred ships of the Anglo–French armada were just approaching the invasion target. Early the next morning the seaborne assault began. British commandos, followed by tanks, landed at Port Said. The French simultaneously launched their operations against the twin town of Port Fuad. Both were captured by the afternoon. An armoured column immediately set off along the road south to the town of Suez. After covering barely twenty-five miles it halted. News had arrived that Britain and France had accepted a ceasefire.

General Sir Charles Keightley, joint commander-in-chief of the allied forces afterwards estimated that by 12 November Suez could have been occupied. But the Cabinet which met on the morning of 6 November made the fateful decision to call off the operation. Domestic opposition was not decisive. The military operation had indeed produced a bitterly divided House of Commons. There were hints of resignations from the government and civil service, but only Anthony Nutting took the plunge on 4 November, followed by Edward Boyle, financial secretary to the Treasury. The nation at large was also as deeply split as at the time of the Munich conference debate of 1938. A mass demonstration in Trafalgar Square on 4 November heard speeches on the theme 'Law, not War'. On his journeys between Downing Street and parliament Eden was booed as often as he was cheered. But he had accepted these consequences as one of the dangers of the operation.

Fear of Soviet intervention was likewise of secondary importance. On 4 November the Soviet army had entered Budapest to suppress an uprising which had erupted at the end of October. Eden could not speak authoritatively about events in Hungary without being accused of diverting attention from Egypt. On 5 November he had received a menacing letter from Bulganin graphically warning that the world was on the edge of another war. This threat was not taken seriously by Eden or any of his Cabinet colleagues.

A more important consideration had been the condemnation of the United States and its pressure exercised through the United Nations. When words appeared to have no effect, Washington used its most deadly weapon – financial blackmail. Losses of gold and dollar reserves, particularly from speculation against sterling in New York, had created a serious situation by early November. The American Treasury, on Eisenhower's orders, refused Britain a loan. The final stab in the back came on 6 November, at the moment the Cabinet was meeting. Macmillan received the news that Washington was deliberately obstructing his efforts to withdraw the British quota of dollars deposited with the International Monetary Fund in order to buy and thus support sterling. The Americans would not agree to the technical procedure involved until the British government accepted a ceasefire. Yet in *Riding the Storm* Macmillan maintained that, serious as this was, it did not determine the decision to call a halt. A conclusive military success in Egypt, so tantalizingly near, would soon have restored the financial situation.

Eden himself first revealed in *Full Circle* what was subsequently confirmed in the memoirs of Kilmuir, Butler and Macmillan. The prime minister wrote: 'We had intervened to divide and, above all, to contain the conflict. The occasion for our intervention was over, the fire was out. Once the fighting had ceased, justification for further intervention ceased with it.' Furthermore, according to Eden, no Cabinet minister suggested continuing the intervention, although it does seem unlikely that during the Cabinet discussions that case was not presented. That was the decision taken, which the French government also accepted, despite the fact that they wanted to capture the entire canal. With Israeli–Egyptian hostilities at an end, Britain and France had no choice but to abide by the terms of their own ultimatum. Its limited declared aim of separating the combatants was the only fatal error.

Now began the Anglo–French retreat from Suez, accompanied

by humiliations almost vindictively inflicted by the United States. Eisenhower had been re-elected on 6 November. He was no longer hampered by considerations of domestic politics or the legalistic ambiguities of Dulles. The president immediately cancelled an invitation, just extended, for Eden to visit Washington. He then demanded an immediate and unconditional withdrawal. For two weeks Eden and Mollet resisted, insisting on the prior arrival of the UN force and a phased withdrawal of the invasion forces. Advance UN units arrived in Suez on 21 November. Eisenhower then moved with implacable determination. The urgent need for oil in Britain and France, where rationing had been introduced, brought on 3 December submission on the issue of withdrawal. On the 22nd the last British and French troops left Port Said. Israeli forces finally evacuated Sinai on 16 March the following year.

This undisguised American pressure served in fact to enhance Eden's popularity. But he was not destined to remain for long as prime minister. His eventual resignation, it must be emphasized, was not related directly to the Suez crisis. Prime ministers do ride storms, and Cabinet unity on the whole, buttressed by the closing of ranks within the Conservative party, would have given Eden strength to carry on through the post-mortem and beyond. Unfortunately in early November Sir Horace Evans, his physician, became anxious about his health. The fever had not returned but there was a danger of the return of his previous bile duct trouble. Furthermore, Eden was suffering from exhaustion arising from the ruthless pressure of events. His physician ordered him to take a complete rest. It was an agonizing decision for Eden. At a time when British troops were in an uncertain predicament he would be out of action. It was only the seriousness of his condition which compelled him, after consulting Cabinet colleagues, to acquiesce. On 23 November he flew with Lady Eden to Jamaica for a rest at Golden Eye, the estate of the writer Ian Fleming. Butler was left to preside at Cabinet meetings. All major decisions were subsequently referred by telegram to the prime minister. But it was Butler who took charge of what he later called the 'odious duty' of negotiating the withdrawal of the invasion force, re-establishing confidence in sterling, salvaging Britain's relations with the United States and the United Nations, and bearing the first brunt of the Suez debate.

The Edens returned from Jamaica on 14 December. The prime minister appeared to be in a confident mood and physically refreshed. In a statement at the airport he spoke hopefully of the formation of the UN peace-keeping force, of how fatal it would have been to allow the Moscow–Cairo axis to develop, and declared 'that we were right, my colleagues and I, in the judgements and decisions we took'. He obviously intended to continue as prime minister.

Parliament had debated the government's policy during Eden's absence. The battle lines of what has become one of the most controversial events in recent British history were already drawn. The critics of intervention condemned what they regarded as the illegitimate use of force against a smaller power. They regarded the reputation and integrity of one of Britain's outstanding statesmen – a conciliator and man of peace all his life – as having suddenly been destroyed. The apologists defended the use of force, complaining only that the operation had been prematurely halted. All had to agree that both the overt and covert aims of the crisis, to internationalize the canal and topple Nasser, had disastrously failed. In retrospect Eden too admitted that he had not been successful in his wider objectives. Yet he drew limited comfort from the fact that the United Nations had at last created a peace-keeping force; a check had been put on Nasser's expansionist ambitions; and the United States had abandoned its complacent attitude to the Middle East. On 5 January 1957 the Eisenhower Doctrine proposed to deter communist aggression by offering economic and military aid to any threatened state in the Middle East.

Both critics and apologists remained intrigued by the question of collusion. What proved to be Eden's last speech in the House of Commons, on 20 December 1956, dealt with this subject. He reminded members that on 31 October Selwyn Lloyd had already denied that Britain had acted in collusion with Israel. The government, Eden continued, had now been asked whether they had had any 'foreknowledge' of the Israeli attack against Egypt. He denied that Britain had engaged in 'some dishonourable conspiracy', and he added: 'there was not foreknowledge that Israel would attack Egypt – there was not. But there was something else. There was – we knew it perfectly well – a risk of it, and, in the event of the risk of it, certain discussions and conversations took place, as I think, was absolutely right.' This was a less than candid remark about a subject on which Eden had spoken for the first and last time.

Eden went to Chequers for the Christmas holiday. There he suffered a recurrence of the fever which had affected him in early October. On the advice of Sir Horace Evans, Eden returned to London for more specialist examination early in the new year. A second and third medical opinion confirmed the grim news. The fever indicated that his internal complaint would worsen, making him incapable of carrying the load of office. Eden realized that he had to resign. He visited the queen at Sandringham on 8 January to tell her of this decision and the medical reasons for it.

The following morning Eden spoke to Butler and Macmillan about his resignation. Macmillan recalled how deeply upset he was at the 'sudden and tragic end to the adventure on which we had set out so gaily some twenty months before'. The two men sat in the drawing-room at Number 10 and talked about World War 1 and politics. At 5 p.m. Eden presided over his last Cabinet meeting. Nothing of his decision had been previously leaked. Speaking with great dignity, he briefly announced his resignation as prime minister. It came as a dramatic shock. Short tributes from Cabinet colleagues followed and the meeting came to an end. Later that evening Eden formally tendered his resignation to the queen at Buckingham Palace. Harold Macmillan's succession to the premiership was announced the next day. Eden stayed for a week at Chequers. On 18 January, a cold and foggy day, he and Lady Eden sailed from Tilbury to spend the winter in New Zealand.

This was the dramatic end to an extraordinary career. On his return to England Eden resigned his Warwick and Leamington seat and retired from public life. Fears for his health persuaded him he should write a first volume of memoirs, although the last chronologically, dealing with the years from 1951 to 1957. It appeared in 1960. In July 1961 he accepted the customary offer to a prime minister of an earldom, taking the title of first Earl of Avon. Having always had more staying power than his appearance suggested, Eden continued writing his memoirs, and two further volumes appeared in 1962 and 1965. Occasional articles and lectures and a rare television appearance in 1974 to reminisce about 'Facing the Dictators' in the 1930s were exceptions to an almost total retirement on a Wiltshire farm. The reputation he had built since 1923 remains identified with the one event – the Suez crisis. It is a cruel fate, even by the harsh standards of politics, to be remembered by one failure and not by numerous achievements.

BIBLIOGRAPHY

PUBLIC RECORD OFFICE
Minutes of the Cabinet, CAB23; Foreign Policy Committee of the Cabinet, CAB27/624–7; War Cabinet, CAB65; and Defence Committee, CAB69. Selected papers of the Prime Minister's Office, PREMI; and the Foreign Office, FO371.

BOOKS BY LORD AVON
Places in the Sun, 1926.
Foreign Affairs, 1939.
Freedom and Order, 1947.
Days for Decision, 1949.
The Eden Memoirs, Full Circle, 1960.
The Eden Memoirs, Facing the Dictators, 1962.
The Eden Memoirs, The Reckoning, 1965.
Towards Peace in Indo-China, 1966.

BOOKS ON LORD AVON
Bardens, Denis, *Portrait of a Statesman*, 1955.
Broad, Lewis, *Sir Anthony Eden*, 1955.
Campbell-Johnson, Alan, *Sir Anthony Eden*, 1955.
Churchill, Randolph S., *The Rise and Fall of Sir Anthony Eden*, 1959.
McDermott, Geoffrey, *The Eden Legacy*, 1969.

Nutting, Anthony, 'Lord Avon', in Herbert van Thal, ed, *The Prime Ministers*, vol. 2, 1975.

Rees-Mogg, William, *Sir Anthony Eden*, 1956.

SECONDARY SOURCES

Background books relevant to Lord Avon's career are too numerous to list. Many have been consulted in the preparation of this biography. The following memoirs, diaries and biographies are particularly informative.

Acheson, Dean, *Present at the Creation*, 1969.

Attlee, C. R., *As it Happened*, 1954.

Birkenhead, Lord, *Halifax*, 1965.

  Walter Monckton, 1969.

Butler, Lord, *The Art of the Possible*, 1971.

Chandos, Lord, *Memoirs*, 1962.

Churchill, Winston S., *The Second World War*, 6 vols, 1948–54.

Dilks, David, ed, *The Diaries of Sir Alexander Cadogan, 1938–45*, 1971.

Dixon, Piers, *The Life of Sir Pierson Dixon*, 1968.

Eden, Robert Allan, *Some Historical Notes on the Eden Family*, 1907.

Eden, Sir Timothy, *The Tribulations of a Baronet*, 1933.

Eisenhower, Dwight D., *Mandate for Change, 1953–56*, 1963.

  Waging Peace, 1956–61, 1966.

Feiling, Keith, *Neville Chamberlain*, 1946.

Fisher, Nigel, *Iain Macleod*, 1973.

Gladwyn, Lord, *Memoirs*, 1972.

Gore-Booth, Paul, *With Great Truth and Respect*, 1974.

Hailsham, Lord, *The Door Wherein I Went*, 1975.

Hare, Sir Steuart, *The Annals of the King's Royal Rifle Corps*, vol. 5, 1932.

Harvey, John, ed, *The Diplomatic Diaries of Oliver Harvey, 1937–40*, 1970.

Hoopes, Townsend, *The Devil and John Foster Dulles*, 1974.

Hull, Cordell, *Memoirs*, 2 vols, 1948.

Hutton, Sir Edward, *The King's Royal Rifle Corps Chronicle* 4 vols, 1916–19.

Ismay, Lord, *Memoirs*, 1960.

Kilmuir, Lord, *Political Adventure*, 1964.

Macmillan, Harold, *The Blast of War, 1939–45*, 1967.

  Tides of Fortune, 1945–55, 1969.

Riding the Storm, 1956–59, 1971.

Madariaga, Salvador de, *Morning Without Noon*, 1974.

Maisky, Ivan, *Memoirs of a Soviet Ambassador*, 1967.

Menzies, Sir Robert, *Afternoon Light*, 1967.

Middlemas, Keith, and John Barnes, *Baldwin*, 1969.

Miller, T. B., ed, *Australian Foreign Minister, The Diaries of R. G. Casey, 1951–60*, 1972.

Moran, Lord, *Winston Churchill, The Struggle for Survival, 1940–65*, 1966.

Muggeridge, Malcolm, ed, *Ciano's Diary*, 2 vols, 1947–52.

Murphy, Robert, *Diplomat among Warriors*, 1964.

Nicolson, Nigel, ed, *Harold Nicolson, Diaries and Letters*, 3 vols, 1966–8.

Nutting, Anthony, *Europe Will Not Wait*, 1960.

No End of a Lesson, 1967.

Pearson, Lester B., *Memoirs*, vol. 2, 1974.

Roskill, Stephen, *Hankey: Man of Secrets, 1931–63*, vol. 3, 1974.

Simon, Lord, *Retrospect*, 1952.

Sherwood, Robert E., *The White House Papers of Harry L. Hopkins*, 2 vols, 1948–9.

Spaak, Paul-Henri, *The Continuing Battle*, 1971.

Strobe, Talbot, ed, *Khrushchev Remembers*, 1971.

Sulzberger, C. L., *A Long Row of Candles*, 1969.

Temperley, A. C. (Foreword by Anthony Eden), *The Whispering Gallery of Europe*, 1938.

Templewood, Lord, *Nine Troubled Years*, 1954.

Tree, Ronald, *When the Moon was High*, 1975.

Trevelyan, Humphrey, *The Middle East in Revolution*, 1970.

Truman, Harry S., *Memoirs*, 2 vols, 1955–6.

Wheeler-Bennett, Sir John, ed, *Action this Day, Working with Churchill*, 1968.

Winant, John G., *A Letter from Grosvenor Square*, 1947.

Woolton, Lord, *Memoirs*, 1959.

INDEX